MADRID 19 FINAL

CHAMPIONS
OF EUROPE

LIVERPOOL LEGENDS

Written by Michael O'Neill

sona
BOOKS

sona BOOKS

First published in the UK by Sona Books, an imprint of Danann Media Publishing Limited 2023

WARNING: For private domestic use only, any unauthorised Copying, hiring, lending or public performance of this book is illegal.

CAT NO: SONO569

Photography courtesy of

Getty images:

Popperfoto	Tony Duffy	Paul Ellis
Bob Thomas	Ross Kinnaird	Tom Jenkins
Nigel Roddis / Stringer	Dave Thompson / Stringer	Stu Forste
Andrew Powell	Laurence Griffiths	Paul Barker
Alex Livesey	Ian MacNicol	Michael Steele
Harry Ormesher	John Powell	David Cannon
Clive Brunskill	Michael Regan	William Vanderson
Ben Radford	W & H Talbot Archive	Christian Liewig / Corbis
Mirrorpix	Icon Sport	Liverpool FC
Fox Photos	Ed Lacey	
Mark Leech / Offside	Evening Standard	

All other images, The Press Association, Wiki Commons

Book cover design Darren Grice at Ctrl-d

Layout design Alex Young at Cre81ve

Copy Editor Martin Corteel

Proofreader Finn O'Neill

Made in EU.

ISBN: 978-1-915343-29-1

CONTENTS

INTRODUCTION

There are few clubs in England that can claim to inspire such deep-rooted emotional attachment in its followers as the Reds from Merseyside, Liverpool FC. Liverpool has nurtured astonishingly talented men and watched them deliver unforgettable, thrilling football; but from among the many there emerge those few with abilities that make them stand out and constantly bring golden football memories. The names of the club's greatest players and managers are indelibly engraved in the hearts of fans not only in the UK but worldwide, the stories of their greatest feats in the service of the club reverberate through the decades.

Delving far back into the club's history, in the following pages we once again meet those players, and the managers who guided them, the crème de la crème of Merseyside, to shine a spotlight on the talent and strength of character that enabled such illustrious men as Billy Liddell, Ian Rush, Steven Gerrard, Ian Callaghan, Kevin Keegan and that modern-day football messiah Mohamed Salah to gain football superstardom.

By distilling the physical skills and mental ability of these men, focusing a light on their speed, their ability to read a game, strength, deceptive ball play or their willingness to embrace the team spirit, thrive on initiative and leadership, we shall learn what it takes to climb to the top echelons of the greatest game in the world.

The men who pace feverishly on the sidelines, the managers, have not been forgotten, either. Without their eagle eyes, sharp game intelligence and ability to form relationships of mutual trust and respect with their players, Liverpool would not have achieved the status it has earned. From the club's first managers, William Edward Barclay and John McKenna, through the glorious years of Bob Paisley and the great Bill Shankly to Jürgen Klopp, who is in danger of becoming a legend during his own term of management, they deserve the appellation of legend to give credit to their powerful contributions to Liverpool's success.

The wealth of talent that has been on display throughout Liverpool's exhilarating past is drawn together here to form a legendary collection of the greatest and never-to-be-forgotten Liverpool FC legends!

View of Kop Stand with new Jürgen Klopp banner displayed before the Premier League match between Liverpool and Everton at Anfield on 20 February 2021

LEGENDS OF LIVERPOOL FC

LEGENDS

I t's a dangerous task, attempting to define what makes a player a football legend, but those we have singled out displayed many, or in some cases all, of the physical and mental attributes that can turn matches on their heads and take spectators out of their seats in admiration.

An exceptional flair, confidence and unbreakable determination are prerequisites, and these men were certainly not lacking in those. They also possessed skills in abundance. But what else set them apart from their teammates?

▼ The Kop end is seen as Liverpool attack Everton during the Barclays Premier League match between Liverpool and Everton at Anfield on 27 September 2014

JOHN BARNES

THE FLAWLESS MIDFIELD MAESTRO WHO ELEVATED LIVERPOOL

Born on 7 November 1963 John Barnes made his Liverpool debut on 15 August 1987 against Arsenal. His first goal came against Oxford United on 12 September when Liverpool won 2-1. He made over 407 appearances for Liverpool scoring 108 goals and was regarded as one of his club's and the country's best players.

▼ John Barnes celebrates with Ian Rush

▶ John Barnes poses in the home team dug-out for an official photograph shortly after signing for Liverpool from Watford at Anfield on 9 June 1987

407 APPEARANCES
108 GOALS

This Jamaican-born midfielder joined Liverpool when racial injustices against players of colour echoed throughout England, to become a favourite with his Liverpool teammates, his club, and also a cultural pioneer.

John Barnes joined the club from Watford in 1987, and donned jersey number 10, which will always be associated with him at the club. Barnes also gained 79 England caps. From his position out on Liverpool's left wing — he was later moved to a midfield role — his matches produced 108 goals for the Reds.

Barnes lived out his career in an era when English

football hooliganism was rampant and widespread racism blighted the English game. Barnes regularly came in for disgusting verbal abuse from the stands. On one infamous occasion during a Merseyside derby at Goodison Park, a photo captured him nonchalantly backheeling a banana someone had hurled his way. As a player of immense prominence — only the second black player to don the Liverpool red, the first to gain a regular first-team place — he became a pioneer through the dignity of his response to prejudice, his refusal to succumb to the bait of his tormentors, to be deterred from his football achievements or allow himself to

◀ Steve Chettle of Nottingham Forest fouls John Barnes for a penalty during the FA Cup semi-final at Hillsborough. Liverpool won the match, 1 January 1988

▶ John Barnes European Football game

overreact to the discrimination he suffered. Thus, he disarmed the braying pack.

Many in Liverpool were sceptical about Barnes's commitment to the club, but he blew that claim out of the water and stated his credentials as a major talent from the start, initially with a virtuoso display against Oxford United, where he worked his magic to set up John Aldridge for the first goal, then capping that with a 37th-minute goal of his own, a beautiful curling left-footer into the net. "Everything I tried worked; every trick or dribble, feint or pass produced something," he said. This he followed up by driving home two goals against Queens Park Rangers in October 1987. First of all with his famed cool head under pressure, he put the ball into the centre of the box for the first goal from Craig Johnston. Then split-second thinking from Barnes with a one-two pass before he gracefully placed the ball into the net past the keeper.

Renowned for his dribbling skills — the ball seemed to be attached to his foot on a bungee cord — Barnes's brilliance was fully displayed in the second goal. After challenging and winning the ball on the halfway line, he took off down the pitch towards goal, unstoppable. Two defenders converged on him, 50 yards of the turf had been covered but Barnes still danced through, Alan McDonald arriving first with a sliding challenge, and then Terry Fenwick tried, only to see Barnes dart away to the right. He maintained his composure and loped

forwards to place the ball into the goal with his right foot once again (he favoured his left foot) between goalkeeper David Seaman and another defender. This was the goal that Barnes remembers as his finest of all time. Better, even, than his remarkable solo run in the international against Brazil in 1984. On that occasion he twisted and swerved his way through the entire Brazilian defence.

Then, with a final feint in front of the goalkeeper, he calmly slotted the ball into the net with a deft one-two, emphasising his ability to use either foot.

The rest of the season passed off in a similar fashion as he sent over beautiful airborne or defence-splitting passes and increased his goal tally.

Kevin Ratcliffe of Everton brings down John Barnes of Liverpool during the FA Cup final at Wembley Stadium in London. Liverpool won the match 3-2, May 1989

With Liverpool, he rapidly achieved success even within the club that dominated English football at the time and thus underlined his status as England's greatest talent. His talent also quieted many of the raucous racist voices among Liverpool spectators and ushered in a sea change in attitudes towards non-white players.

Ironically, Barnes's arrival marked the tail end of Liverpool's glory years in the 1970s and 1980s, although Barnes would help them to two Division One championships, two FA Cup wins and a League Cup win in 1994-95.

He proved his rise to greatness with his all-time best statistical performance for Liverpool in one season, which came in the 1989-90 season, with 22 league goals and 5 FA Cup scores. One League Cup strike brought his total that season to 28 as he helped Liverpool to the league championship for the 18th time. Barnes equalled his Liverpool debut season tally (1987-88) in 1990-91 with 16 league goals and one FA Cup goal.

This was also the season when he was moved to a midfield position, a change that went practically unnoticed, but a role in which Barnes proved to be devastatingly effective. His confidence allowed such audacious feats as the bending free-kick against reigning champions Arsenal (against whom Barnes scored twice that season) in November 1989.

In his heyday, Barnes could instantly propel his six-foot frame with powerful acceleration. Imposing and impressive physicality did nothing to interfere with his technical skills, his supple and elusive dribbling, his accurate passing, all of which created a footballer seen "once in a generation in English football up to that point", according to the press.

Robbie Fowler praised his erstwhile teammate;

"I don't think I've ever seen a more talented player in training… There were things he could do that you used to stand up and applaud. Sometimes, his presence alone would win matches for Liverpool, because he could dominate the opposition. He never gave the ball away, and in training he could do absolutely anything."

Opposition players just couldn't get him off the ball or off his feet, his sense of balance was remarkable and the opposition players would bounce off his solid frame.

Defender Jamie Carragher was another teammate who Barnes impressed: "Technically, he's the best player I've ever trained or played with. He was great with both feet, they were both exactly the same… I'd say he's the best finisher I've ever played with. Barnes never used to blast his shots — they'd just get placed right in the corner. You speak with the players from those great Liverpool sides and ask them who the best player they played with was and they all say John Barnes."

▶ John Barnes in action

No stranger to spectacular performances, Barnes was blisteringly prolific when at the top of his form. He might sprint in a short burst into the penalty area, or strike from short distances after appearing unexpectedly in a space. Entire defences were left floundering in his wake before he executed a clinical finish or, remembering the 4-4 FA Cup classic against Everton in 1991, he would dart in from the left and loft the ball over into the far corner. If in full flight, he was virtually impossible to catch, and if he saw a flicker of a chance, as against Southampton in 1996, he took it, slicing the ball accurately through every defender across one-third of the field into the net. Chips, drives, lobs over defensive walls, scissor kicks, Barnes could pull anything out of the hat when the occasion demanded it, earning him the unique epithet, "unplayable".

Barnes won the Football League First Division twice, the FA Cup twice and the League Cup and Charity Shield once. He was a member of the team that won

▲ Division One, Liverpool 2 v Queens Park Rangers 1. John Barnes celebrating with Alan Hansen and the other Liverpool players as the team win the League Championship, 28 April 1990

▶ John Barnes Barnes in full flight for Liverpool against Sheffield Wednesday, 1995

the Football League First Division PFA Team of the Year three times, was voted PFA Players Player of the Year in 1988 and was voted FWA Footballer of the Year in 1988 and 1990. He became an MBE in 1998 and was inducted into the English Football Hall of Fame in 2005. On 6 September 1995, Barnes, the extremely talented and graceful player who played exciting, fast-moving football, won his 79th and last international cap for England.

In 1992, Barnes sustained an injury to his Achilles

tendon, which signalled a period of difficulty, visible in his performances. This led to his being cast aside by manager Graeme Souness.

Only in 1994-95 did he again make 38 appearances. The barrel-chested Barnes was returned to a prominent role in manager Roy Evans's 3-5-2 system. Now heading into his mid-thirties, Barnes found a new lease of life. His Pandora's box of passing skills, ability to guide the flow of the game and his intelligent reading of the game was back in use in a midfield role that suited his diminishing athleticism and did not demand the speed required of a winger.

In his final season in 1996-97 in which he only missed three Premier League games, and having scored seven goals in all competitions — although he made seven appearances in European games — it was time for the torch to pass on even though many still considered him the best player in the club at the time. Three months before his 34th birthday it was over. On 13 August 1997 having been with the club for 10 years and 407 appearances, 108 goals and five major trophies, "Digger" Barnes, (he acquired the nickname from the character Digger Barnes in the American TV soap opera *Dallas*) moved on with a free transfer. Barnes retired from playing in 1999.

The Liverpool fans honoured their adored player by naming him fifth in the poll of "100 Players Who Shook The Kop".

IAN CALLAGHAN

A JEWEL IN THE GOLDEN-ERA CROWN

Born on 10 April 1942, Ian Callaghan joined the club as an apprentice on 28 March 1960, playing his first match for Liverpool on 16 April. He was a regular in the team from 1961 onwards and also played for England as a member of the World Cup-winning team in 1966.

▲ Ian Callaghan in action

▶ Ian Callaghan takes on Phil Beale of Tottenham Hotspur during a Division One match at White Hart Lane

857 APPEARANCES
68 GOALS

Joining the Liverpool side in 1959, coming in just before the famous Bill Shankly took over the reins to reshape the team that had been struggling to get back out of the Second Division, Ian Callaghan became a star in the new manager's road to Liverpool success and in the subsequent golden years of the 1970s.

Born in the Toxteth area of Liverpool in 1942, Callaghan's talent began to shine in the 1950s as he showed his quality as a potential star in Liverpool's schoolboys teams of the 1950s.

Liverpool FC decided to take him on and he signed with them as an apprentice at Anfield. The youngster became one of those who would pass through a Liverpool apprenticeship and emerge in the first team and as an England international.

The young player had also also caught the eye of the great legend of Liverpool at the time, Billy Liddell, his boyhood hero, who said of him: "There is a 17-year-old called Ian Callaghan, who looks like taking over from me. I played with him twice, watched his progress, and I believe he'll be a credit to his club, the game and his country."

And so it proved.

Shankly also saw Callaghan's potential and put him in the first eleven at Anfield within a fairly short time frame, so Callaghan's debut arrived on 16 April 1960 in a home game against Bristol Rovers in which the Reds were victorious with a 4-0 scoreline. The newbie contributed to three of the four goals. That win came just six days after his eighteenth birthday, and Liddell's predication came true, for the youngster had replaced him.

"For Liverpool, right-winger Ian Callaghan," read an article in the *Daily Express*, "a veteran of four Central League games, just ended the most accomplished league debut I've had the pleasure to witness."

Spectators gave the young man a standing ovation, as did players in both teams and the referee.

It was to be the first of 857 games for the club until 1978. Ever after, Callaghan would speak of his manager in passionate terms that revealed his love and respect for him.

Because of Callaghan's power and speed, which enabled him to overcome defenders, reach the byline and then fire a cross over from the line, Shankly placed him wide out on the right at Liverpool.

It was the 1961-62 season, when Liverpool were challenging for the Second Division title that saw Callaghan transcend from beginner to veteran in 23 appearances. He was in the team on the day the team gained promotion, 21 April 1962, after a 2-0 win against Southampton.

Now a regular in the first team, as he was for the next 15 years, he formed a dangerous duo with Peter Thompson over on the left. The terrible twins were in the team that won the First Division in 1964 including a memorable 3-0 win against Manchester United in which Callaghan scored the first and sent a cross to Alf Arrowsmith's head for the second.

The relentless attacking play that had brought him great admiration and established him as a top winger was evident when he put away the two goals in Liverpool's crucial 2-1 win over reigning champions Everton in the 1964-65 season, Callaghan's statistically best season, as he assisted on nine goals and scored eight having played in every league game of the season. Only in the 1968-69 season would he score more goals. He needed all of that determination during Liverpool's first-ever FA Cup victory, 2-1 against Leeds United.

◀ Ian Callaghan, Liverpool midfielder, ahead of the English League Division Two match between Leyton Orient and Liverpool at Brisbane Road in London, England, 17 March 1962. The match was drawn 2-2

Callaghan had put the Reds through in a fifth-round match at Bolton Wanderers with just six minutes left to go after he had seen a possibility open up. Thompson chipped him the ball and Callaghan headed it in.

When the scores drew level in the final, it was Callaghan who sped to the byline in one of his classic moves, past two defenders and sent in a low driving ball to beat the defence and reach the head of Ian St John, whose goal gave the Reds a deserved victory. He considers that his most memorable moment: "… Liverpool lifting the FA Cup for the first time. It was also my first appearance at the stadium and I had a hand, or

rather a foot, in the winning goal."

In the 1965-66 season that saw Callaghan score five goals, the club came out on top of the league again, although the burst of silverware was then over until 1973. But Shankly had no doubt about what Callaghan meant for Liverpool: "Ian Callaghan is everything good that a man can be. No praise is too high for him. He is a model professional, and a model human being… you could stake your life on Ian. Words cannot do justice to the amount he has contributed to the game. Ian Callaghan will go down as one of the game's truly great players."

Despite the team's lack of trophies, Callaghan continued to produce his searing runs down to the byline.

Following a season when he scored an all-time best of 10 goals, 1968-69 Callaghan's appearances almost halved in 1970-71 after a knee injury; his days of skipping past defenders on the right flank and floating lethal crosses into the middle for the forwards were over. But when Shankly then moved him to midfield, a new lease of life opened up and kept him playing for another seven years. In midfield he could use his intelligent reading of a game and make use of his astonishing work rate. An ideal position now that his pace was no long what it had been.

Callaghan set a new record of appearances for Liverpool and crowned his successful career to that

Callaghan makes a burst forward with the ball, 1967

Ian Callaghan with Bob Paisley after Liverpool's victory in the 1977 European Cup Final

time by breaking Billy Liddell's long-standing club record of 534, on 15 August 1972.

Callaghan, renowned as the consummate professional and a man who looked after his teammates, now began a second and even more successful chapter in his career with Liverpool. Six years overflowing with titles: the league in 1973, 1976 and 1977; the FA Cup in 1974; the UEFA Cup in 1973 and 1976; and the European Cup in 1977; and a substitute in the 1978 European Cup.

Before Bob Paisley succeeded Bill Shankly in 1974, the team gave the old boss one last moment of greatness: Anfield in May 1973 when Callaghan would help his manager achieve another of his promises — that one day all of Europe would have to take notice of Liverpool.

At Anfield in May 1973 — the year Callaghan received the FWA Player of the Year award — Liverpool took on Borussia Mönchengladbach in the UEFA Cup

final. Callaghan was deployed in both legs of the final on the left the midfield three together with Peter Cormack and Emlyn Hughes, and a glorious night ended with Liverpool 3-0 winners. It was enough to give them the cup, despite a 2-0 defeat in Germany.

Paisley invested the same faith in Callaghan as Shankly had done. The player was now 34 years of age, his achievements greater than most players could

experience and vision. He guided the game flow with long passes and through balls to the centre-forwards or the wide midfielders, while he could move into the wide areas to send over the wonderful lofting balls that were his trademark.

Nonetheless, by 1977, it was evident that the passing years were having an effect and his sharpness and pace were noticeably diminished; his passing, reading of a game and accurate long crosses kept his career alive, as the forwards continued to benefit from his presence. The number of his appearances dropped from over 40 to 33.

In his last season for the club, 1977-78, Callaghan went onto the pitch just 26 times, although he got the call from England manager Ron Greenwood to play against Switzerland on 7 September.

But the end was looming, and in a semi-final tie of the European Cup against Borussia Mönchengladbach, Callaghan wore the red shirt for the last time as Liverpool battered the German team, again 3-0.

For a total break with the past, he then went to US team Fort Lauderdale Strikers on loan.

Ian Callaghan spent his entire Liverpool career without being booked or sent off except in his penultimate game for Liverpool in March 1978 when his name went into the book.

Callaghan confessed that although his disciplinary record was exemplary, he had in his own words, "got away with murder", on occasion and mused that he would be booked in every game he played in today's world.

In his 18 years at the club, he appeared in a record-breaking 857 games, won the League title five times, the FA Cup twice, the European Cup twice, the UEFA Cup twice and the UEFA Super Cup once.

dream of at his age; he'd been capped for his country — although, oddly, just four times — and been part of the 1966 World Cup-winning squad. And although retirement was just four seasons away, he would score goals in every one of them.

His role as central midfielder alongside players such as Emlyn Hughes or Alun Evans, highlighted the seamless working of his technical expertise, skill,

KENNY DALGLISH

THE MAN WITH THE MAGIC TOUCH

Born in Glasgow on 4 March 1951, Kenneth Dalglish boasted a career that lasted 22 years from the moment he was picked for the Scottish U-15 national team. He arrived at Liverpool in 1977 fresh from his successes at Scottish club Celtic, where 321 appearances had brought him 167 goals. In 2009, FourFourTwo magazine named him as the greatest striker in post-war football in Britain.

▲ Kenny Dalglish leaps high to control the ball, as Manchester United's Mike Duxbury makes a challenge, Milk Cup Final, Wembley, 26 March 1983

515 APPEARANCES
172 GOALS

▲ Kenny Dalglish, Wolves v Liverpool, 27 August 1983

Kenny Dalglish, brought in to replace Kevin Keegan, played his first match for Liverpool on 13 August 1977 in a Charity Shield 0-0 draw against Manchester United. His first League goal came one week later after just seven minutes against Middlesbrough and was captured by the *Liverpool Echo*: "The first goal of the game came appropriately enough from the £440,000 feet of Kenny Dalglish... it stemmed from a lovely, down-the-middle move as Case controlled the ball, flicked it through to McDermott who turned into the path of Dalglish... and Dalglish strode smoothly on to beat Platt comfortably as the goalkeeper came out. It was a perfectly finished shot."

Dalglish scored in his first four games, and ended his first season at Liverpool as top goalscorer with 31 goals in total to his credit, one of which was the sixth goal in a 6-0 drubbing of Hamburg in the second leg of the 1977 European Super Cup.

One year later came one of the forward's most memorable goals as he dashed forward through the defence to calmly flick the ball over the keeper and secure a 1-0 victory against Club Brugge in the 1978 European Cup final.

In 1978-79 Dalglish scored 10 including a brace when Liverpool beat Tottenham Hotspur 7-0 at Anfield, which is still today considered one of the greatest games in the club's history. Dalglish twisted 180 degrees to whip the ball into the net for his first, and showing his unerring hunter instinct was able to take a misfired Liverpool shot and flick it into the net in a fraction of a second. His quick mind and feet were also involved in almost all of the other moves that ended in goals. In 1979, with 56 goals after two seasons helping the club to another league title, and as top goalscorer again, he was named Football Writers' Association Footballer of the Year. Dalglish was now considered the best player in Britain.

Famous for his feints, Dalglish would, for example, graze the ball with his right foot while feigning a move to the left before instantly cutting back to the right to charge forwards for one and a half yards with his opponent flailing behind him. An entire generation of footballers found themselves unable to contend with the swift-footed forward.

Ian Rush made his debut in what would be a terrible 1980-81 season for club, although the Dalglish-Rush partnership would prove to be the great spearhead of the Liverpool attack. For Dalglish, 16 games without a league goal from late November to the end of the season represented a crisis. Dalglish then suffered an ankle injury in April that put him out of action.

The minor crisis continued, however, when Dalglish failed to score in the first nine games of 1981-82. Then, against Brighton on 17 October 1981, the 11-month drought in the League came to an end when he scored after 12 minutes. By the end of the season he had put away 13 goals in 42 matches.

▶ Kenny Dalglish during the FA Charity Shield against Everton, 18 August 1984

Liverpool were league champions again as they would be in the following two seasons. Dalglish, whose brilliant passing made him the linchpin of the side, was recognised for his talent and given the PFA Players' Player of the Year award and the FWA Footballer of the Year award.

Emerging from their success in the league, the League Cup and the European Cup and with Joe Fagan now in charge, in 1983-84 Dalglish struck his 100th goal, which arrived after 241 games in the Liverpool

red. In a 1-1 draw with Ipswich Town in November 1983, Dalglish saw a gap and dashed forward to the take a short corner for Liverpool, turned, dispensed with the defender challenging him, and with his trademark right-left feint struck a superb left-foot shot high into the far corner of the net. This was the season he also surpassed Denis Law's scoring record with his 15th goal in the European Cup in September.

A broken cheekbone kept him out of 14 games in 1984, but at the age of 33, he was considered valuable

◀ Dalglish and the other Liverpool players and coaching staff celebrate with the European Cup, 30 May 1984

post just one week before the infamous European Cup final at the Heysel Stadium in Belgium against Juventus. Thirty-nine Juventus fans died in a crush.

Joe Fagan had gone. Dalglish insisted that Bob Paisley be with him for the first two years as player-manager. Dalglish rose to the task, the dual role, and guided the Liverpool squad to its first double, in the 1985-86 season. The League Championship fell to them by two points thanks to a winning goal by Dalglish in a victory over Chelsea on the final day of the season. It was again a classic performance showing the player-manager's spatial awareness and razor-sharp reactions when he positioned himself perfectly, wrong-footing the defence in the box, took the ball on his chest and struck the ball past the keeper without letting it touch the ground.

The FA Cup fell to them in a 3-1 victory over Everton.

Although some questioned the suitability of Dalglish as player-manager, he would guide the team to further successes, becoming one of Liverpool's most successful coaches with three more league titles and two FA Cup wins to his credit.

"People are a bit frightened of him. He growls at them, he makes them jump," reported one Scottish newspaper.

And another story shows Dalglish's down-to-earth attitude. When his secretary, Sheila, asked him if he wanted a new desk, Dalglish said that he took a look around his office. Then he replied: "This was Bob's desk, this was Joe's chair. Why would I need new ones? … Just put a bar in, Sheila." Which they did.

enough to be offered a four-year contract. Then, in 1985, Dalglish's history was set on an unexpected course.

Having been dropped for the first time in his career in October the year before, Dalglish was back in November to score his 30th and final goal in the Scottish national side, thus equalling Dennis Law's record. He received an MBE for his services to football in the 1985 New Year Honours List. And then, as an absolute affirmation of Dalglish as an indispensable part of Liverpool's success, he was offered the managerial

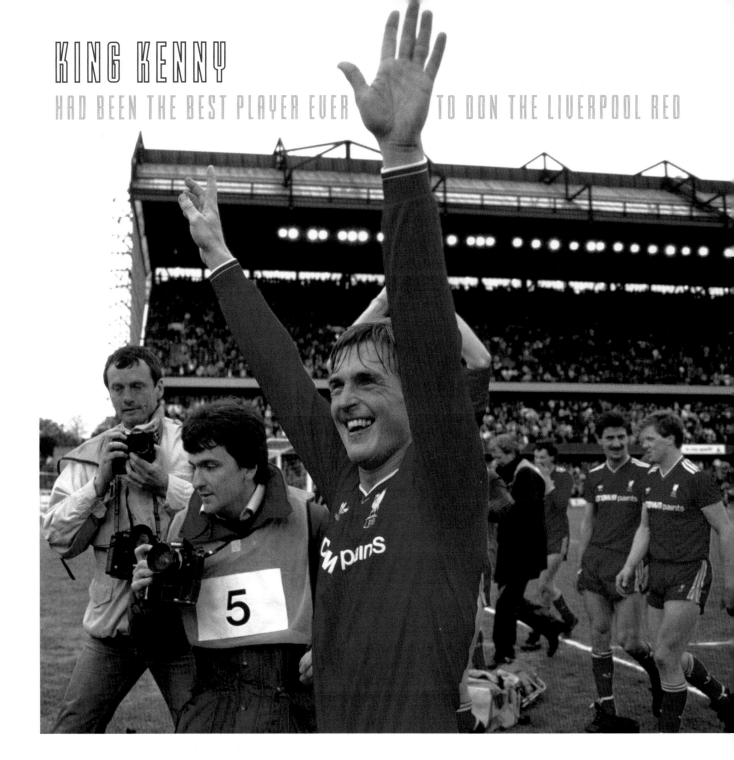

Dalglish's stature was enhanced, his behaviour described as, "colossal and heroic", in the aftermath of yet another tragedy to strike Liverpool when the team played Nottingham Forest in Sheffield on 15 April 1989. The surging crush of spectators claimed 97 lives in total. The "fearsome" manager revealed his humanity and emotional connection when he attended many of the funerals, on one occasion four in one day. There were suggestions that his exemplary behaviour

after Hillsborough, outstanding playing and managerial career, combined with the charity work for breast cancer support, merited his being given a knighthood. He was profoundly affected by this acknowledgment of his engagement in all the spheres of his life.

Having picked up the Manager of the Year award for the third time in five years, Dalglish called it a day. Not having been a regular in the team since October 1986, he ran onto the pitch for the last time in Merseyside red

◀ Liverpool player-manager Kenny Dalglish celebrates winning the First Division Championship after a 1-0 victory over Chelsea at Stamford Bridge, London, 3 May 1986

▼ Liverpool Football Club's new manager Kenny Dalglish poses for photographers during a photocall at Anfield, 10 January 2011

in the penultimate game of the season, for a 1-0 victory against Derby on 1 May 1990.

And then, on 22 February 1991, came the moment many dreaded. Dalglish stunned Liverpool by resigning.

"Although I didn't realise it at the time, Hillsborough was the most important factor in my decision to leave Liverpool in 1991," he wrote many years later.

Dalglish returned to manage the side as caretaker manager in 2011 and then on a three-year contract. His second term was short-lived and controversial and his defence of Luis Suárez when the player was banned for abuse towards a Manchester United defender and seemed to refuse to shake hands with Evra in the return match, did nothing for the manger's reputation.

By the following year, Dalglish's star, although burnished by success in the Football League Cup and defeat by one goal in the FA Cup final, had been irreparably tarnished by the team's eighth-place finish in the league. Dalglish was dismissed on 16 May 2012.

Both Bill Shankly and Bob Paisley thought that Dalglish, King Kenny, had been the best player ever to don the Liverpool red. "Of all the players I have played alongside, managed and coached in more than 40 years at Anfield, he is the most talented. When Kenny shines, the whole team is illuminated."

Those were Paisley's words. And Shankly? " … Dalglish wants to get on, but I would have moved heaven and earth to keep him. I would rather have quit and got out of the game altogether than sold a player of his brilliance."

Kenny Dalglish made 515 appearances for Liverpool and scored 172 goals for the club. He won the Ballon d'Or Silver Award, was voted top of the Liverpool fans' "100 Players Who Shook the Kop" poll, in 2006. Dalglish has been inducted into both the English and Scottish Football Halls of Fame.

STEVEN GERRARD

A GENIUS MIDFIELDER WHO DEFINED LIVERPOOL'S DOMINATION

Born on 30 May 1980 in Whiston, Merseyside, Steven George Gerrard, MBE, was spotted by Liverpool scouts while playing for the Whiston team. At the age of just nine, he joined the Liverpool Academy, only leaving Merseyside to go to LA Galaxy in 2015, after 17 seasons with the Liverpool squad.

▲ Steven Gerrard applauds the fans after his last game against Stoke City at Britannia Stadium, 24 May 2015

710 APPEARANCES
186 GOALS

◄ Steven Gerrard folds off Ian Harte
of Leeds during the Liverpool v Leeds
United FA Carling Premiership match at
Anfield, 13 April 2001

The man who Zinedine Zidane and Pelé considered to be the best footballer in the world scored 186 goals for the Reds in 710 appearances in which he helped the team to cup glory in Britain and Europe.

The 6ft (1.83m) midfielder's debut for the club came on 29 November 1998 against Blackburn Rovers, and as his talents rapidly matured, he made his debut for the England squad in 2000 and became Liverpool captain in October 2003.

Steve Gerrard's first professional contract arrived in 1997; with Liverpool, of course, and in that first match against Blackburn Rovers he came on as a late substitute. The player recalled that he was out of position and out of his depth. Yet from this humble start,

12 appearances in his debut season, he began to make his presence felt in midfield. He experienced a difficult beginning caused by back problems that his sudden spurt of growth had brought about. Nonetheless, Gerrard was chosen as captain of the Under-18s and then for the Under-21 England national side in September 1999, and was able to demonstrate his versatility in the season that saw him utilised as a right-winger, right-back, a left-back, and a defensive and offensive midfielder.

The first goal for the club, arriving on 5 December 1999 against Sheffield Wednesday in a 4-1 win, proved to be a goal of such class and quality that the *Liverpool Echo* went into overdrive in its descriptions of: "A wonderful talent, a young man with the steel of a Stiles and the style of a Souness, sidestepped, danced and dribbled past three defenders before finishing decisively."

Such was the impression that he made that he was chosen to be part of the England national squad on 31 May 2000. And as the 2000-01 season rolled around, he was beginning to score goals with more regularity, 10 that season. It was a bumper season for the young Gerrard, the season that he won major honours with Liverpool for the first time, helping them to bring home the FA Cup, the Football League Cup and the UEFA Cup, won after a 5-4 thriller final in which Gerrard scored in the 16th minute. He considered it his best goal; it was a beautiful action in which Gerrard read the flow of play perfectly and rocketed through the defence into the open gap behind to pick up the pass, move forward with it and absolutely thunder a low shot into the net.

Gerrard's star continued to rise, despite Liverpool's own star sinking somewhat and the silverware becoming much scarcer. "I was captain of my school side, and I used to go along to Anfield to watch the

team. I used to watch Barnes with the captain's armband and dream that one day it would be me captaining the team I love."

As he was to spend almost his entire career with Liverpool, his dedication was beyond dispute. Gerrard once said: "When I die, don't bring me to the hospital. Bring me to Anfield. I was born there and will die there."

▲ Steven Gerrard drives the ball through the wall during the match between Liverpool and Middlesbrough in the FA Carling Premiership at Anfield, 20 January 2001

◀ Gerrard pictured in 1999

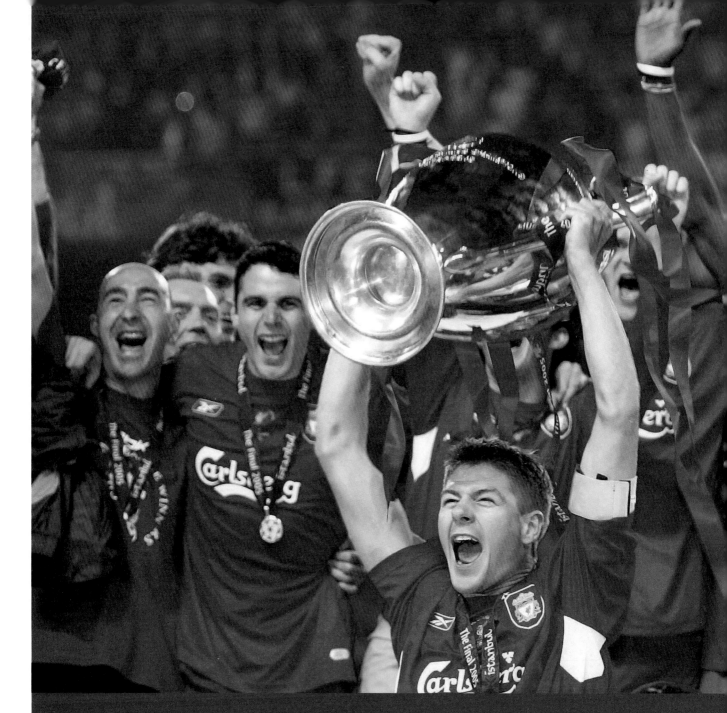

That dedication and the indefatigable talent that saw him claim another goal in the League Cup final win against Manchester United in 2003, brought him the captaincy of the team on 15 October 2003, proving how much his presence was valued and his stature had grown.

He proved to be a great leader; his tackling was strong, his passes were canny and pinpoint accurate as befitted his excellent reading of a game, and when he struck the ball it cannoned from his foot, which led to terrific goals. Simply put, he was a brilliant all-rounder

and that put him on par with other legendary Liverpool heroes such as Billy Liddell and Kenny Dalglish.

Liverpool were unable to change their fortunes in the league even when Rafael Benítez took over as coach for the 2004-05 competitions. Gerrard's contribution, however — he was joint goalscorer that year with 13 — was enormous. Yet the club hesitated to renew his contract, a career low point for Gerrard. He proved the insanity of the absent thought processes in the boardroom, when in the UEFA Champions League qualifying match against Grazer AK; Liverpool won 2-0

◀ UEFA Champions League Final, 25 May 2005, Ataturk Stadium, Istanbul, AC Milan 3 v Liverpool 3, (Liverpool won 3-2 on penalties). Liverpool captain Steven Gerrard celebrates with the trophy

hit son! What a hit!" At the time, Gerrard felt this to be perhaps his best goal for Liverpool.

Even more extraordinary was what happened in what came to be known as the "Miracle of Istanbul" in May 2005 in the UEFA Champions League final. Three-nil down, this was the moment every Liverpool fan expressed undying love for Gerrard's extraordinary talent. When he rose above the AC Milan defence to place a perfect header in the net, he showed of what calibre leaders are made.

When he was about to score Liverpool's third in this incredible comeback story, he was brought down in the box, Liverpool went level and eventually won the penalty shoot-out. "Lifting the cup as Liverpool captain was just the best moment of my life," were Gerrard's words.

In the 2006 FA Cup final, which went down in Liverpool history as the Gerrard final, Liverpool faced West Ham and were 2-3 down in the 54th minute. The ball ran back to Gerrard, who with yet another mighty, stunning volley drove the ball through the defence across almost one-third of the field and into the net. He hit it from there, he said later, because his feet weren't able to carry him any further. He was voted man of the match.

By season's end, Gerrard had claimed 23 goals for Liverpool for the first time ever.

Liverpool's fortunes waned in the years that followed, and by 2009, it was clear the Gerrard's best years were behind him. Yet his talent was so honed, that he still picked up awards, voted Liverpool Player of the Season for 2009, Premier League Player of the Month for March 2009.

courtesy of two goals from Gerrard, the first a curling cracker that steamed into the net from a strike from outside the area when he saw the half chance. Then, hovering lethally unmarked in the box, he slammed in the second low along the ground.

He repeated his feat in the 86th minute of Liverpool's Champions League match against Olympiacos in 2004 when he was left unattended in midfield and with a thundering 25-yard volley made it 3-1. The TV commentators were almost lost for words at the perfection of his shots: "Oh, you beauty! What a

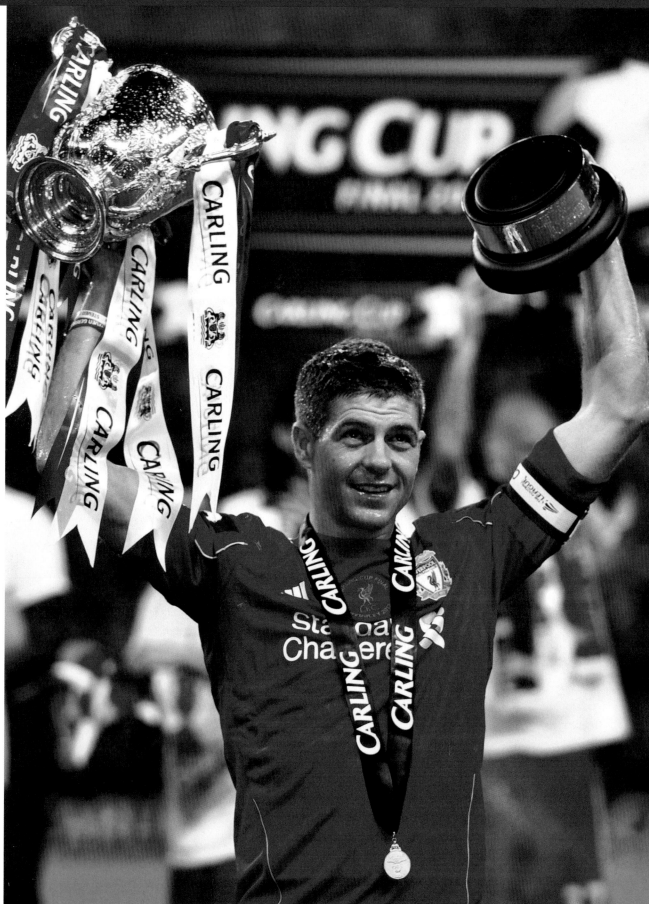

Even though he missed a penalty in the shoot-out, Liverpool were able to take home their first trophy for six years when they won the 2012 Football League Cup final against Cardiff City. Gerrard beamed with delighted relief.

That year, Gerrard became England captain in his own right as well, winning two Man of the Match awards and his 100th cap in November joining the elite ranks alongside Bobby Charlton, Bobby Moore and Billy Wright. He would eventually reach 114, having made his debut on 31 May 2000 at the age of 20 and played his last match on 24 June 2014, when he was 34 years of age, his first goal arriving against Germany on 1 September 2001.

Brendan Rodgers was in charge at Anfield in 2012-13, and he decided to slot the now 32-year-old Gerrard into a new "holding" role just in front of the back four in midfield to compensate for his diminishing physical capabilities. It was just another in the many changes of position that he had experienced and did not put him off his stride; far from it. He adapted in his inimitable way and successfully helped the club challenge for the Premier League.

Gradually, his physical ability to speed forward and assist in an attack declined, and he attempted fewer long-range strikes at goal.

By 2015, the longest-serving skipper in the club's history had decided to call it a day. He departed the club at the end of the season. His indelible legacy to the club was in the performances that brought moments of magic to the field: none more dramatic than when he carried out his runs through defences into the penalty area or slammed in his high-voltage volleys.

Held in high regard for his leadership skills and for inspiring confidence in his teammates, also for his steely determination and influence on the pitch, Steven Gerrard was determined, second to none in his passing ability and his tackling skills, a man singled out by fate to be one of the greatest footballers of his age.

Gerrard married Alex Curran on 16 June 2007. He has received 27 personal awards, many of those he received on multiple occasions.

◀ Steven Gerrard celebrates with the trophy after his team beat Cardiff City to win the League Cup Final at Wembley Stadium in London, 26 February 2012

▶ Gerrard in August 2014. The 2014-15 season was his last for Liverpool

ROGER HUNT

THE PHENOMENAL FINISHER WHO PROPELLED LIVERPOOL'S TRIUMPHS

"To be the goalscoring catalyst of the Shankly team, to achieve promotion then win those precious league titles and the FA Cup put him in the bracket of LFC legends who are responsible for making us the club we are today." Thus was Roger Hunt honoured by Jürgen Klopp.

▶ 1960s football card featuring Roger Hunt portrait and signature

▶▶ The 1966 FA Charity Shield Merseyside derby match between Liverpool and Everton at Goodison Park. Picture shows, Roger Hunt and Ray Wilson, members of the summer's victorious England team, parading the World Cup trophy around the stadium before the game

492 APPEARANCES 285 GOALS

Another of those players whose dedication to the team resulted in them spending almost their entire careers with Liverpool FC, Roger Hunt, dubbed "Sir Roger" by the grateful Liverpool fans, joined Liverpool in 1958 and would stay with them for the next 11 years. When he left in 1969, he had become the club's record league goalscorer with 244 goals and also gained 34 England caps claiming another 18 goals on the international stage.

It was on 9 September 1959, over one year after he had joined them, Hunt was promoted to the first team. Liverpool were playing in the Second Division against Scunthorpe United and Hunt was given the chance to stand in for Billy Liddell. In his debut game, the forward scored his first goal at Anfield, running onto a pass in the 64th minute and striking the ball into the net. There

▲ Roger Hunt scores despite the efforts of Spurs goalkeeper Hollowbread and right-back Ron Henry, 27 March 1964

▶ Roger Hunt hurdles Norman Hunter of Leeds United in the 1965 FA Cup Final

was no doubt that he would certainly be able to replace Liddell, who was nearing the end of his career, but Hunt was ready to admit that the Cheshire League had been inadequate preparation for professional competitions.

Hunt wasn't considered to be an orthodox centre-forward, but his ball control and footballing skills could be fully utilised by deep positioning. When Bill

Shankly took over the Liverpool reins in December 1959, Hunt became a vital cog in Shankly's rebuilding of the Liverpool team and ended the season as top goalscorer.

Liverpool were soon challenging for the top spot, and by the end of the 1961-62 season, Hunt had scored an all-time best goal tally of 42 goals, scoring a hat-trick in the third game of the season against Leeds United (when he let loose a signature long-range shot to score Liverpool's fifth) the first of five that would seal his claim to greatness that season. The team were promoted.

Hunt would become top goalscorer for Liverpool for eight consecutive seasons, the arrival of Ian St John being the spark that ignited Hunt's already obvious talent. Hunt described their brilliant partnership as, "almost telepathic". Over the next four seasons, Hunt would hit the back of the net 129 times.

In 1964, renowned for his physical strength, his swiftness of foot as well as the dynamism of his shooting, Hunt was having the time of his life and hit home 31 league goals that season. The team finally won more silverware with the championship title, and in 1965 came what was possibly his greatest achievement to date, his performance in the FA Cup final of 1965 against Leeds.

Hunt had scored four in the run-up to the game, but now the tussle went into extra time. Hunt, lurking in front of goal, placed himself perfectly for a header into the net to revive the team's flagging spirits before St John headed in the winner.

In the year that Liverpool won the league title again, 1965, Hunt's 29 league goals brought him selection for the England 1966 World Cup team, and he again proved invaluable scoring against Mexico and twice against France to put England through to the knockout stage. The goals were classic Hunt.

Hunt was lurking in front of goal again, first to slot in a rebound and then he sailed up to a cross to head in his second. Playing in the final meant that he had played in all six competition games and scored three times, a testament to his talent.

The vital importance of Roger Hunt's contribution to their teams was understood by both Shankly and England manager Ramsey. His flexibility meant that he could adapt to two very demanding managers and their varied styles, both of whom were therefore able to fully exploit the striker's intelligence. With Liverpool, he was well supplied by both Peter Thompson and Ian Callaghan, which meant that he could benefit from the width he was allowed. But Ramsey's "wingless wonders" also benefited from his presence.

Hunt rose to prominence in an era in which his modest and reserved character would be able to produce close friendships with other footballers. As a result, his style of play was in keeping with his character and gained less attention than the more flamboyant Jimmy Greaves, for example. And yet, only twice in 34 international outings did he find himself on the losing side, his contribution to that record unchallengeable. And England captain Bobby Moore understood the striker's qualities: "Roger Hunt is a players' player. He is possibly appreciated more by those who play with him and against him than by those who watch him."

"I knew perfectly well that I wasn't an out-and-out natural, the sort who can make a ball talk, so it was down to me to compensate for it in other ways," Hunt

◀ Roger Hunt (second left bottom row) pictured with the Cup-winning 1965 Liverpool team

▶ Roger Hunt at Anfield July 1968

is reported to have said, adding, "I threw myself into training, ran and tackled for everything and practised my ball skills at every opportunity."

For Hunt, the silverware feast with Liverpool was over except for his first goal of the 1966-67 season in the Charity Shield in a 1-0 defeat of rivals Everton. But in the league, Hunt's tally of goals dropped to 14 which still made him top goalscorer.

He increased that the following season and secured his place in Liverpool FC history by becoming the club's record goalscorer. In the game, the 8-0 rout, against TSV 1860 Munich of West Germany, Hunt scored his 242nd goal on 7 November 1967. His second that day was a beauty to behold, as the match report read: "For skill and subtle deception, Roger Hunt's second goal a minute later was a connoisseur's effort. Three defenders were left on the ground as Hunt twisted inside the six-yard box and after deceiving Radenkovic calmly aimed his left-foot shot into an unguarded net." Hunt already held the record of scoring 100 top-flight goals faster than any player in Liverpool's history.

Liverpool fell three points short of the champions, Manchester City, that year, but Hunt boosted his goal tally to 30 and proved to be the lone scorer in 10 of the games.

For gentleman Roger Hunt, as his thirties came upon him, the writing was on the wall for his time with Liverpool.

was given an inch of ground he was one of the world's most dangerous players, scoring goals from every angle, some seemingly impossible, with calculating precision. Because so many of Hunt's magnificent goals seemed so relaxed, his talent appeared to pass unnoticed; yet it was the very fact that he made those goals seem so easy to score that proved how immense his talent was. The goal that he put away in the European Cup semi-final against Inter Milan in 1965 is a case in point. Hunt spurted forward into the open spaces he always seem to find, to pick up the cross that came over parallel to him, then twisted and struck the ball first time without hesitation leaving the goalkeeper with his arms helplessly by his side. "His style and control, not only on scoring goals but in killing the ball dead, stamped him as a player," said Bill Shankly.

His importance and legacy for Liverpool's ascent from the Second Division to the Premier League championship has been described as second to none, in tandem with Bill Shankly. Hunt was one of Liverpool's superstars.

In 1969-70, it was clear that Hunt, along with his veteran teammates, were no longer producing the desired results. A fifth-place finish in the league with rivals Everton winning the championship, a defeat by Watford, a Second Division club, in the FA Cup and early departures from the League Cup and Fairs Cup competitions, showed that something had to give. To his credit, Shankly started Hunt as his first choice, but by autumn Phil Boersma had taken over.

Hunt gave the club his final goodbyes, firstly in September with two goals against Southampton in the league after he had been taken off the subs bench in the 75th minute. Two more classic goals within two minutes of each other, taken calmly and lethally after he had created spaces for himself through an intelligent reading of the game, were his and Liverpool's reward. Those were his last league goals for the club.

Seventeen goals, in the 1968-69 season, was a meagre haul for him, yet he maintained his top goalscorer spot. But Shankly's frustration at the team's inability to capture the league title or hold some silverware was to see Hunt start to slide off the manager's radar. Perhaps the player was sensing that as well, for in March 1969, when Liverpool were struggling in the FA Cup replay against Leicester City, Shankly took Hunt off for a substitution. An angered Hunt pulled off his shirt and hurled it towards the dugout. This from the gentleman player, who had won admiration for his calm demeanour, was nothing short of a sensation.

Considered one of the best finishers in the game, Hunt's razor-sharp but always cool-headed reactions in front of goal were born of a rare talent. "One of the great goalscorers for Liverpool FC," said Ian Callaghan; if he

And then came the finale, against Vitória de Setúbal in November; Hunt saved the day again with the third goal on the 90th minute, the best goal of the match, as the *Guardian* reporter noted.

When December came around, Roger Hunt was no longer wearing the Liverpool red, but after 285 goals in all competitions had moved to play for Bolton Wanderers.

Hunt's overall scoring record for Liverpool was broken by Ian Rush, although his league haul of 244 goals still stands.

Roger Hunt was awarded an MBE in 2000. The Kop's "Sir Roger" passed away in 2021.

▼ A tribute to former footballer, Roger Hunt, who recently passed away prior to the Premier League match between Liverpool and Manchester City at Anfield on 3 October 2021

KEEGAN

KEVIN KEEGAN

Born on 14 February 1951, Kevin Keegan made his debut for Liverpool on 14 August 1971, originally as a midfielder. With little interest for him from other clubs, Shankly realised that he'd found an exceptional talent and Keegan signed for Liverpool, morphing from a Division Four player to a football superstar of the 1970s and 1980s.

KEVIN KEEGAN

ENG

◀ Kevin Keegan England football card

▶ Kevin Keegan playing against Tottenham Hotspur
— League Division One, December 1971

321 APPEARANCES
100 GOALS

KEVIN KEEGAN

◀ Kevin Keegan tenaciously tussling for the ball

▶ Keegan takes the ball past Dave Clement of Queens Park Rangers

and he took just 12 minutes to prove that he was worthy of the honour and struck his first goal. True, he mis-hit the ball, but his performance throughout left no doubt that here was a star in the making. Keegan kept up the momentum with a tally of three goals in the first five league fixtures. He was already attracting headlines that included the word "magic" to describe his play. By the time of his third goal in the 3-2 defeat of Leicester City, his determination to succeed was so intense that as he thundered in towards the goal to score he followed the ball and managed to get himself wrapped up in the goal netting and had to be untangled. "What a player that is," said an admiring TV reporter. Keegan was a first team regular for the rest of his Liverpool career.

"I was just as sure of Keegan as I was of Denis Law," said Bill Shankly in 1971, "and I never had cause to think again about Denis. These two players are so much alike in number of ways. Keegan is an exciting boy all right."

Keegan had to wait until January 1972 to grab his first brace of goals in a 3-0 win against Oxford United in the FA Cup.

In 1972-73 Keegan began to excel himself, even though it was almost a month before he saw his first goal, in a League Cup fixture. But then five goals were put away in six games.

That season was given a golden glow for Keegan when he gained his first international England cap for a World Cup qualifier with Wales in Cardiff on 15 November 1972. He was 21 years and 9 months of age.

Having scored four goals in a practice match, Kevin Keegan was given his first outing against Nottingham Forest at Anfield for the opening game of the league season in 1971 in the number 7 shirt. The youngster was deployed as a partner for John Toshack with whom he developed an instinctive professional understanding,

He became top goalscorer with 22 in his bag and helped to bring Liverpool the League Championship for the first time since 1966 with his last goal of the league season, when he put away Liverpool's second, lurking in the centre of the action and pouncing onto a goalkeeper fumble to cheekily take the ball away and seal the win against Leeds United in the penultimate game.

On 10 May, Keegan scored twice again in a 3-0 win over Borussia Mönchengladbach in the UEFA Cup final and Liverpool took the prize. Toshack and Keegan combined talents when Keegan flew into the air to head the ball far into the net from halfway in the penalty area. He then blotted his copybook by fluffing a penalty.

But it was Toshack who fed Keegan the ball again as Keegan hurtled in to grab the half-chance and thump in the ball in his inimitable fashion before crashing to the ground.

Keegan put his all into every game, his powerful legs able to perform delicate chips or thundering shots from a distance and his energy levels were extraordinary. His skill in dribbling and his feints and his thrusting runs earned him the nickname "Mighty Mouse". They also made him one of the trickiest players for the opposition to deal with. Keegan's former fitness trainer at Scunthorpe United, Jack Brownsword, could attest to his protégé's commitment: "The thing that impresses me most about you is that you're a hundred percenter," he told the young player, who, even

after everyone else had gone home, would run up and down the terraces with weights tied to his waist.

There was more success in the 1973-74 season in which Keegan was on the field for all of the 61 competitive games, the man for the dramatic occasion. Silver arrived in the form of the FA Cup, and he became top goalscorer again for the second successive season, with 19 goals.

Two strikes against Doncaster Rovers saved Liverpool's bacon in an embarrassing 2-2 draw against his hometown South Yorkshire club, who languished at the bottom of the Fourth Division.

In the semi-final, he rocketed a volley past Leicester City's Peter Shilton and then scored two in the final against Newcastle. Not waiting for the defence to close him down, his first was a cool-headed powerful volley. He continued to harry the defence, tenaciously tussling for every ball until he waited in a gap fight in front of goal to slot in Liverpool's third. His awareness of positioning, as always, dangerous for the opposition.

Bill Shankly moved on. King Kev must have felt the change personally, and would soon make a decision to move on also. "Shankly loved Kevin like a son," was Ian Callaghan's opinion. "They adored each other. Bill made everybody feel special. He didn't like to play favourites with players, but their bond was clear."

In another rare occurrence, Keegan managed to blot his copybook again before the 1974-75 season had properly started. In the Charity Shield match, won by Liverpool — now guided by Bob Paisley — 6-5 on penalties. Keegan was punched in the face in a horrible assault by Leeds United's Johnny Giles, and then a furious Keegan and Billy Bremner were sent off, removing their shirts as they left. Both were charged with bringing football into disrepute. Rather ironic as Giles had only escaped after Keegan had asked the referee to treat the Leeds man leniently.

No more honours came his way that season. But from that point on until he left, he and the club would be showered with silverware.

Season 1975-76 brought the league title and the UEFA Cup in its goody bag. Keegan again coming up with a crucial goal against Leicester in the league for a 1-0 victory — as Liverpool became champions by just one point. His strike in the vital game against Wolverhampton Wanderers with the game trudging towards a title-losing 1-0 defeat, flooded the team again with new life.

◄ Ian Callaghan, Kevin Keegan and Ray Clemence parade the trophy after the 1974 FA Cup Final between Liverpool and Newcastle United at Wembley. Liverpool won the match and final 3-0, 4 May 1974

▼ Charlie George Derby County gets to grips with Liverpool's Kevin Keegan at the Baseball Ground, League Division One, 28 February 1976

With 15 minutes left to play, Liverpool were on the edge of the abyss. Again the terrible twins were at work. Toshack with the most delicate of headed passes as Keegan came hurtling into the penalty area scything into a gap and with a right-foot tap put the ball past the keeper. This was Keegan, fighting hard, and proving again how difficult he was for opposition defences to pin down.

He crowned the magnificent season with a penalty to save the day again in the UEFA Cup final against Club Brugge in the first leg and score the equaliser in the second; the final score 3-2 in Liverpool's favour.

Keegan became top goalscorer once more the following season as he and the club reached another pinnacle with the double of the league and the European Cup. His performances were described as "irrepressible". He ran himself into the ground during the game against Borussia Mönchengladbach in Rome, and German defender Berti Vogts was ground down by his forceful play. With just eight minutes left to play, Keegan set out on a typical run starting 40 or so yards out, reaching the penalty area where Vogts' foul was all that ended his

◀ Keegan walking out for a game against FC Zürich in 1977

▼ Kevin Keegan was far more than just a pin-up boy

charging attack. That led to another Liverpool goal.

But everyone knew that he was playing his final season, for halfway through the competitions Keegan dropped the bombshell that he was moving to Hamburg. With offers coming in from all over Europe, he chose to move to Germany, where he would harvest yet more honours. The failed FA Cup final against Manchester United was his last game for the club, and after 323 appearances and 100 goals, and assisting in 72 more, he was replaced by Kenny Dalglish.

Kevin Keegan won three First Division titles at Liverpool, one FA Cup, one European Cup and two UEFA Cups. He became European Footballer of the Year in 1978 and 1979. He was capped for England 63 times and scored 21 goals and captained the team.

He had become a celebrity superstar at Liverpool and knew how to exploit his popularity commercially in the media. The former England captain had revolutionised the footballer's status, but he proved to be far more than just a glamorous pin-up boy, although he was, and Liverpool's first, in fact. Keegan was one of the most talented and enthusiastic players at the club, generous in his playing, making great chances for his colleagues with intelligent passes, and he is remembered as one of the finest players to run out onto the Anfield pitch. As dangerous in the air as on the ground, his combination of intelligence, sharp reading of the game and speed were astonishing to watch, his untiring enthusiasm was infectious and inspirational for his teammates. Everything he had done for the club and his teammates from the moment he arrived at Anfield to the moment he departed, he had, "… done with enthusiasm and passion". The squad were instantly impressed by Keegan's determination, said Ian Callaghan, "His enthusiasm and energy were fantastic from the off … a very fit young guy and he gave everything — you could see how much he wanted it."

BILLY LIDDELL

MERSEYSIDE'S FIRST LEGENDARY PLAYER, WHO WON HEARTS, MINDS AND GAMES

Born on 10 January 1922, for the Liverpool supporters of that era Billy Liddell is simply the best player ever to run out in a red shirt. Yet he almost didn't. He was studying to be an accountant, and only at the behest of half-back Matt Busby did Liverpool employ the man who became a legendary player.

▶ Billy Liddell from Scotland and Outside Left for Liverpool Football Club running with the football prepares to pass during the English League Division One match against Fulham on 29 October 1949 at the Craven Cottage stadium in Fulham. Liverpool won the match 1-0.

◀ Billy Liddell pictured in 1955

534 APPEARANCES
228 GOALS

It was 27 July 1938 and Billy was a teenager when he started his Merseyside career while continuing his studies, at his parents' insistence, as they wished their contemplative and scholarly son to go to university. He trained just twice a week with the youth team, finally becoming a professional in 1939, although his studies continued and he was employed part-time at a firm of accountants.

When he damaged his knee playing football, it seemed that his career had prematurely ended; the Second World War intervened, however, and Billy Liddell enlisted as a volunteer in the RAF, emerging a skilled navigator and pilot. He was still able to play for local clubs and for Scotland in an amateur international, and he drew immediate attention, already mentioned as a "maestro class" player and "the war's best find", his skill on the ball attracting great admiration. He played eight times as a Scottish international during the war, scoring on his debut in a 5-4 win over England in 1942 with a "lovely timed header".

Finally released from the RAF, in 1946, Liddell could put those skills in the service of Liverpool in his first game, an FA Cup tie against Chester on 5 January. He would never play for any other team and was still at the club 15 years later.

Liddell was now 24 years of age, and played on the left wing and although he was not yet at the peak of his fitness, he was already an essential part of the team as even the press noted: "Liddell means so much to his side". Liddell put the ball away once in two appearances in his debut season, but in just a few years he would become top goalscorer and repeat the feat seven times. He was able to celebrate Liverpool's fifth league title in 1947. And then the club entered a difficult period when nothing seemed to go right for them.

Liddell was the lone scorer in two games in the 1947-48 season that saw the club fall to 11th in the

league and then 12th in 1949. But Liddell shone throughout, never more so than against Arsenal in September 1948: "Liddell had played outstandingly on many occasions but never before with such brilliance, and when he took up Jack Balmer's beautifully placed through pass to hit a grand goal… the Arsenal crowd rose up to him," enthused the press with, "Liddell was brilliant", headlines. This was the season when Liddell could be seen as a left-back and in four different forward positions as well. By the end of his career he had played in 10 different roles.

In a season in which Liddell was a lone scorer in four league matches and became top goalscorer for the first time, 1949-50, he also helped the club to come closest to silverware, scoring a vital goal on 5 March 1950 in the FA Cup. It was his only chance at goal and he took it in magnificent style, hurtling onto a through pass to thunder the ball into the net.

Liddell was on the spot again in the semi-final to help in the 2-0 defeat of Everton; but the final went to Arsenal, although Liddell displayed flashes of brilliance when permitted and was described as the only man that deserved to save the game for Liverpool. Never again would he get the opportunity to play an FA Cup final game for the club, and the team's fortunes went from bad to worse.

Three more seasons with Liddell as top goalscorer passed, to no avail. It was Liddell who was able to break a 10-match run without a win in 1950, when he picked up a short pass and outwitted the Chelsea defenders to fire in a cracker shot for the only goal. After slipping to 17th place in the 1952-53 season, Liverpool were relegated in 1954, a season in which Liddell had just

seven goals to his credit. Liddell was the star of the club, but without support, his talents were underused or wasted but never in doubt. Bill Shankly gave his opinion on Liddell's abilities: "Liddell was some player… He had everything. He was fast, powerful, shot with either foot and his headers were like blasts from a gun. On top of all that he was as hard as granite. What a player! He was so strong!"

In their first season in Division Two, they almost fell down another rung, but a late rally, with Liddell firing in 30 league goals, dragged them out of the danger zone. Liddell also put away a multitude of penalties, including two for his hat-trick against Fulham when he

was brought down, then running the ball into the net for another goal, and he scored twice in three other matches.

Known as a quiet man, Liddell was a gentleman both on and off the pitch: "He was the friendliest and most approachable guy I think has ever been at Liverpool," said one of the players in later years. Described as a visionary, no less, a once-in-a-lifetime player, the esteem in which he was held by the fans was as clear as the words, "Liddellpool, Liddellpool!" that echoed from the Kop. His commitment to the club at that difficult time was extraordinary; he stayed faithful although he could have picked almost any other club to join.

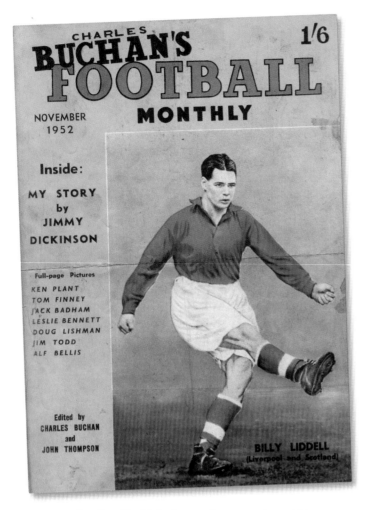

CHARLES

BUCHAN'S

FOOTBALL

MONTHLY

1/6

NOVEMBER 1952

Inside:
MY STORY
by
JIMMY DICKINSON

Full-page Pictures
KEN PLANT
TOM FINNEY
JACK BADHAM
LESLIE BENNETT
DOUG LISHMAN
JIM TODD
ALF BELLIS

Edited by
CHARLES BUCHAN
and
JOHN THOMPSON

BILLY LIDDELL
(Liverpool and Scotland)

◄ Billy Liddell on the cover of Charles Buchan's Football Monthly, November 1952

Another Scottish player who remembered him mentioned that Liddell had the type of build that made him visually seem strong and speedy. "You thought, just by looking at him that he had a good chance of pushing the ball past the full-back and beating him for speed and that was really his game." He was more likely to "get up the line and whip the ball across for his teammates or cut inside for a shot at goal — and he could do either," in preference to waiting for short passes inside. Wherever he played, he was a constant danger to the opposition.

Despite Liddell being on fine form during the second year in the lower division and firing home a personal best of 32 goals, the club could only manage third place in the 1955-56 season.

Liddell was promoted to captain and added to his reputation with a hat-trick against Nottingham Forest with three memorable goals, finding space and shaking off a defender for his first. He continued to work like

a Trojan and gained his second when he turned the ball into the net from a very narrow angle, completing his trio with a "brilliantly headed goal", reported the *Liverpool Echo*.

Liverpool were third again the following year, challenging for the league title without ever quite managing to crack second spot and gain promotion although Liddell was finding the goal frequently, as right-winger and inside-right, top goalscorer for three years in succession.

Changing times were just around the corner for club and player, however, as the 1957-58 season got under way. In November 1957, Liddell took over from Elisha Scott and achieved a record 430 league appearances.

Liddell's age was now evident in his play, his pace slowing, which brought an alteration in his tactics and more considered passes to his game. The challenges for club glory fizzled out and fourth in the league was all that came the team's way.

A sign of the impending finale came in 1958-59 when he was omitted from league and cup lineups, although he claimed another record by taking the top club goalscorer honour. And he was again left out of the side for the opening game of the next season. But he proved he was far from down and out by sending the ball home twice in the second game. Nonetheless, the team struggled until Bill Shankly arrived in December. But Liddell was then beset with injuries, although Shankly continued to value him and use him in the team.

Liddell's final goal was struck in a 5-1 defeat to Stoke City in March 1960, his final game was in August 1960.

Liddell's greatest triumph for the Scottish team came in 1952 during the Home Championship competition against England at Wembley. Bobby Johnstone had scored Scotland's first from a cross by Liddell and with the game 2-1 in Scotland's favour, Liddell was close to the action to pick up a dropped shot from Billy Steel to drive the ball home from 12 yards. Although England pulled one back, that goal turned out to be decisive and earned Scotland the title.

Billy Liddell was 39 when he retired and had appeared 534 times for the club he loved, claiming 228 goals and winning 29 Scottish caps. He was a much loved and admired member of the team, known for his good behaviour and professionalism on and off the field, a man who took his religion seriously and never smoked or drank alcohol. The former Liverpool captain

Donald Mackinlay, said of him: "Liverpool have had some good club players, but I think he is the finest in their history... He is one of the greatest club men ever to have played football."

In his later years, Billy Liddell suffered from Parkinson's disease and died in a nursing home in Liverpool at the age of 79 on 3 July 2001.

▼ Billy Liddell leads out the stars for his testimonial match at Anfield with Tom Finney and Bert Trautmann following on, September 1960

PHIL NEAL

THE LIVERPOOL HERO WHO REDEFINED THE MEANING OF RESILIENCE

Phil Neal arrived in Liverpool from Northampton Town for the 1974-75 season, the first signing by Bob Paisley, who had been very impressed by the right-back's performances. Neal was 23 years of age when Paisley asked him how he would like to go to Liverpool. Neal's worries about his future were over.

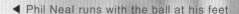

◀ Phil Neal runs with the ball at his feet

▶ 3 May 1980, Liverpool v Aston Villa. Phil Neal plays the ball as Graeme Souness and Aston Villa players look on

PHIL NEAL

It was 16 November 1974 and Phil Neal entered the Goodison Park arena for his debut match for Liverpool, inserted into the side as left-back and about to experience his baptism of fire in red in a Liverpool-Everton derby.

Yet just one hour before kick-off, he didn't even know that he was going to be chosen for the squad. The enormity of the occasion made for a hesitant beginning, but then he proved his value to the team. It was the start of a career that would see him lay claim to his own piece of Liverpool history by scoring more

than once in the European Cup and Champions League finals for Liverpool.

Just one month later he was in the team to face Luton Town at Anfield for his home debut, and from then on he would go from strength to strength to become the most decorated player for the club. And between that game and September 1985, he would miss just one match. He played 22 games that season, usually standing in for left-back Alec Lindsay, and the Reds just missed out on the league title, second to Derby County by two points.

◀ Alan Kennedy and Phil Neal of Liverpool celebrate with the trophy after the European Cup Final victory over Real Madrid in Paris, 27 May 1981

▼ Phil Neal scores the first goal for Liverpool from the penalty spot with Birmingham City's keeper David Latchford going the wrong way, 5 February 1977

It was a different story the following season, 1975-76, when Neal wore the red shirt 42 times in the league, originally returned to his more familiar right-back position before being asked to swap to the other side again, and put away seven goals in total as Liverpool rose to take the top spot again. From then on he would score in every season until he left the club. His first goal went in in November 1975 against Real Sociedad in the UEFA Cup, the last one in a 6-0 rout. Two more goals came against Arsenal in December, again penalties. It was a sign of Paisley's faith in him that he was allowed to step up for those important moments. In fact, Neil would go on to take 38 penalties for the club, missing 13 of them but netting some crucial ones along the way such as the semi-final of the European Cup, FA Cup and League Cup and the 1977 European Cup final.

March saw the defender gain his first England cap in a 2-1 victory over Wales. And this was the season, too, when the Liverpool team with Neal won the UEFA Cup final against Club Brugge and brought Neal's first full season to a magnificent end on 19 May. From now on, he would be back on the right-hand side of the field.

His teammate Ray Clemence valued Neal highly: "Phil adds an extra dimension to the team with his ability to search forward and set things up… he's got a tremendous awareness of every other player in the side and what their job is… add to that his defensive qualities and the fact he's no mean performer in the air and you've got a very good player indeed."

Neal acquired the nickname Zico, the name of a former Brazilian midfielder, one of the greatest players of all time.

That name was well-deserved as his initiative and daring were always on display and never more evident than when he scored his first of two goals in the European Cup competition against FC Zürich, the first a non-penalty goal that he fired in with a beautiful volley after charging in to pick up a free-kick and even the scores. His second came from a penalty, when he coolly wrong-footed the keeper to slot the ball into the empty corner of the net. Then in the final against Borussia Mönchengladbach in May 1977, he was called upon once again to face the guillotine; a penalty to secure the 3-1 win. "As I ran up to the ball," he recalled, "I then did something I never did and which you should never do — I changed my mind. Instead, I hit it low to the other side of the keeper but it went in and up came Cally in delight. I still get a tingle when I see the videos of Bob Paisley and Ronnie Moran and the lads leaping up off the bench with joy."

◄ 9 August 1980, Wembley Stadium, FA Charity Shield, Liverpool v West Ham. Phil Neal and his Liverpool teammates celebrate with the trophy

in the penalty area and picking up a mis-kicked ball pounded it from a sharp angle high into the net.

He also put away four penalties in the league, but the title slipped from the team's grasp.

Paisley had given the defenders Neal and Alan Kennedy the freedom to go on the offensive, although not at the expense of defensive duties and they exploited their new roles to the full.

While at club level Neil used his freedoms to move forward as much as possible to bolster Liverpool's midfield and attack, Neal's style of play in the England squad came in for criticism; with manager Ron Greenwood in particular, his role was more conventionally defensive.

Neal ensured that Liverpool stayed as tight as possible at the back with the result that they conceded only 16 goals and just four at Anfield for the 1978-79 competitions. He helped them win an 11th league title, his five goals contributing to wins totting up a record 68 points, his two lone goals winning the game against Southampton. In another of his signature thundering drives, he put the Reds ahead and any doubts in the press about his ability were dissolved by a "comprehensive player". He could not be restrained to operating at the rear in that game, and with 11 minutes to go surged forward to pick up the ball from Terry McDermott then take it into the penalty area before unleashing another goal.

Feats not to be repeated the next season when he scored just one goal; but he and the team picked up another league title nonetheless, the twelfth in its 88 seasons of existence.

Unfortunately, Neal missed out on an FA Cup winner's medal when the team lost to Manchester United; he would never get a second chance with the Reds.

Neal was instrumental in the European successes of the following season; the European Super Cup when Liverpool defeated Hamburg, and in the European Cup again in 1978 against Club Brugge. He scored twice on the way to that final, the second a magnificent goal against Benfica when he lurked daringly and unnoticed

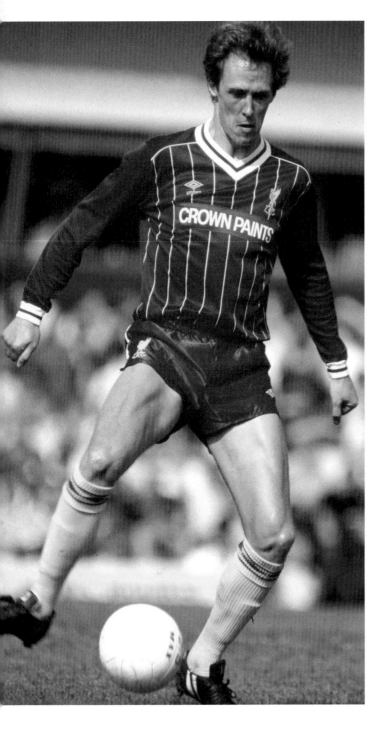

◄ 5 May 1984, Division One, Birmingham City 0 v Liverpool 0. Phil Neal in action for Liverpool

► 31 March 1985, Division One, Liverpool 0 v Manchester United 1. Phil Neal outjumps Manchester United's Jesper Olsen to win the high ball

By the end of 1980-81, a third European Cup and League Cup were tucked away. Neal's most important league goal came in the game against Birmingham City and helped the Reds off the ledge of defeat. In the European Cup matches, he joined the 4-0 romp against Aberdeen. Hurtling forwards on the attack, he scythed down the right behind the defence to take a touch from Kenny Dalglish, move across goal and push the ball in

with his left foot for number two. It was thrilling football, a thrilling finish. The TV commentator made the greatest compliment when Neal took the ball: "… and Neal will score!" implying that once he had the ball the goal was certain.

On final day, Neal made sure the Real Madrid attack was blunted, while still taking every opportunity to be part of an attack, creating dangerous situations and managing to fire in shots even from half-chances. On more than one occasion he blocked the Madrid offensive, helping Liverpool to a 1-0 victory and a third European Cup.

Neal found himself elevated to senior member of the Liverpool team after a sticky start to the 1981-82 season, and Paisley's integration of a swathe of new players. Neal found himself in a mentoring role. He must have been a good mentor, for Liverpool claimed doubles in the two following seasons with the league and League Cup honours falling to their surges.

As 1983-84 came around, Neal was handed the vice captain role under a new manager, Joe Fagan, in a spectacular season that saw Liverpool take the League Championship, the League Cup, and the European Cup. A fourth European Cup and a fourth League Cup winners' medal, made Phil Neal the most decorated player in Liverpool's history.

With three goals that season, none of them was more important than when he scored the opening goal of the 1984 European Cup final against AS Roma. His fearless daring paid off for, having found a large gap around the penalty spot when the ball rebounded from the Roma keeper's head, Neal pounced to drive the

ball home with his right foot between two defenders. As Roma equalised later, that goal enabled the penalty shoot-out and another accurate Neal penalty helped secure a Liverpool victory.

Graeme Souness left at the end of that season and the captaincy was handed to Neal. November 1984 marked the 10-year anniversary of his debut at the club.

Joe Fagan handed in the towel. Phil Neal and new manager Kenny Dalglish found it difficult to come to a rapprochement and Neal began to question his future. When fellow defender Alan Kennedy was sold and Neal

suddenly found himself on the reserve bench for a trip to Everton, it was evident that the door was about to close on his career at Liverpool.

After just a few more games for the club, in December 1985, it was over. Neal accepted an offer to become player-manager of Bolton Wanderers.

Phil Neal won the Football League First Division with Liverpool eight times, the Football League Cup four times and the European Cup four times. He claimed winner's medals for the UEFA Cup, the UEFA Super Cup, and the Football League Super Cup.

IAN RUSH

THE GOALSCORING WIZARD WHO MADE ANFIELD SPARKLE

One of the top strikers in English football during the 1980s and 1990s, Ian Rush was born on 20 October 1961 in Wales. His Liverpool debut came on 13 December 1980 in a 1-1 draw against Ipswich Town. The FWA Footballer of the Year award was handed to him five times.

◀ A young Ian Rush

▶ 1986 FA Cup Final, Wembley, 10 May 1986, Liverpool 3 v Everton 1. Liverpool's Ian Rush takes the ball around Everton goalkeeper Bobby Mimms on his way to scoring his first goal

660 APPEARANCES
346 GOALS

◄ January 1982. Liverpool's Ian Rush is presented with his Matchman of the Month Award

Liverpool first became aware of the player as a 13-year-old, and he signed for Paisley's team when he was nineteen. Already marked out for greatness, he was in the first eleven for his second game, the League Cup Final replay. His first season produced frustratingly gradual results without any goals, and he struggled until his 10th appearance, which arrived in a European Cup first round, second leg tie at Anfield in 1981. Rush was a 64th minute substitute in the game against Finnish side Oulu Palloseura. But his drought ended — and the Ian Rush legend began — three minutes later when he scored from close range in a 7-0 Liverpool win.

Two more goals came from his boot when he appeared against Leeds United at Anfield on 10 October 1981. His ascendant talent as a forward saw him play in all but two of the remaining league games, 49 appearances in all competitions, and he proved an unstoppable goalscorer netting 30 times before season's end. This talent would see him become top goalscorer eight times, Liverpool's all-time leading goal-gatherer.

Spoken of as a "complete centre-forward" — earning himself the nickname, "The Ghost", for sneaking up behind defenders — his fast pace and intelligent reading of a game enabled him to find dangerous positions from where his finishing, with either foot, would be lethal. Kenny Dalglish and he formed one of the most renowned partnerships in Liverpool and European history. Dalglish's passes would often be the start of the excitement, but Rush was capable of retaining the ball to wait for support to arrive or of holding up opposition offensives by harassing the defenders.

Rush claimed his first top goalscorer honour with 31 goals in the 1982-83 season and won all Liverpool hearts with his four-goal performance in the derby against Everton. Racing through from the left, he cheekily tapped in the first, his ninth of the season. His low deflected drive was his second, and then his charge down the field with the ball from halfway saw his strike hit the post and then the net as he followed up with another left-foot drive for the first hat-trick in a Merseyside derby since 1935. It was a brilliant example of how he terrorised defences for Liverpool by making a move long before the opposition saw him and taking the passes to speed onto legendary success.

One week later his second hat-trick appeared against Coventry City, then Notts County suffered the same fate in a 5-1 Liverpool victory at Anfield. Rush was handed the Professional Football Association's Young Player of the Year Award.

Rush's third league championship title and third League Cup fell to him in 1983-84 in perhaps his best season, which he started with three goals during the first four league games. Even better was to come as he put home five to destroy Luton Town in a 6-0 win in October. Three more were added to his tally at Aston Villa in January 1984 and four against Coventry in a 5-0 walloping in May.

Rush picked up the European Golden Boot and the First Division Golden Boot that season.

1 April 1981. Ian Rush holds aloft the League Cup trophy surrounded by fans

An injury put him out of action for two months the following season; tellingly, Liverpool failed to gain any silverware at all.

Back on form in autumn 1985, he netted 33 goals for the season, reserving his finest hour for the FA Cup final against Everton on 10 May 1986. In classic Rush style, he powered forwards into space onto a through ball in the area between defender and keeper to slide the ball into the net. Just before his second, he was lurking in a yawning gap behind the unaware defenders again to pick up the pass and fire the ball into the net for Liverpool to take the honours. Rush considered this to be one of his most memorable games and he took home the Man of the Match award.

On this high note, Rush announced that he was leaving Liverpool to join Juventus, although he stayed a Red for another season and silenced detractors with 40 goals, his second highest tally for the club.

The stay with the Italians proved short-lived. Rush fared less well against the Italians' defensive tactics and illness added to injury made the British striker's stay less than effective. When Rush felt that he was going to be dropped from the team for the following season, it was time for him to leave.

Rush was back at Liverpool for the 1988-89 competitions, although with only 24 appearances his goal tally dropped to 11. He had to adapt so that fellow striker John Aldridge and he could work smoothly together, but

◀ Ian Rush makes his second debut for Liverpool after returning to Anfield after playing for Juventus in Italy, walking out prior to the Mercantile Credit Football League Centenary Trophy match against Nottingham Forest, 29 August 1988

▶ 20 May 1989, FA Cup Final at Wembley, Everton 2 v Liverpool 3 (after extra time). Liverpool striker Ian Rush scores the winning goal past the despairing dive of Everton goalkeeper Neville Southall

missing three months of the season because of a knee operation slowed the process down. When he came on as substitute in the FA Cup final against Everton again, he showed that the old spark was back.

It was a superb swivel shot that started the display, Rush under pressure from the surrounding defenders but hammering the ball into the net in the fifth minute of extra-time. And the winner came from his head when the cross floated in beside him and with a perfectly placed low-gliding header he gifted Liverpool the Cup.

When Rush was given preference over John Aldridge, criticism from the team's top scorer of the previous season piled up, which Rush blunted with 26 goals at the end of the 1990 competitions gaining his

fifth league title, which turned out to be his last.

Meanwhile, he was still turning out for the Welsh international side. Continued success brought him what was considered to be his most famous goal for Wales, which came in 1991 against world champions Germany. The low drive to the left of the goalkeeper was another classic of its kind. The longer he kept possession of the ball the more deadly the danger for the opposing team became, a fact which seems to go against conventional football wisdom. His ability to retain a cool head when under pressure and therefore maximise his fraction-of-a-second decisions turned him into a striker who would punish anyone whose concentration lapsed for even a moment.

Rush claimed top goalscorer spot for 1990-91, and in an otherwise thankless season for the club that hadn't improved much by the summer of 1992, one saving grace was the FA Cup, which went to Liverpool as the team slumped to sixth in the league. Fighting for the cup against Sunderland, Rush found acres of space in front of goal when he took a pass and made it look simple to stay calm and slot the ball home past the diving keeper. His fifth goal in an FA Cup final.

However, Rush turned out for the side just 18 times, a first indication that the tides had turned.

Injuries took their toll on his performance levels, although he managed 32 appearances in the 1992-93 campaign. He achieved a record with his 287th goal in a 2-2 draw at Manchester United; the top goalscorer on

just 14 goals he was unable to push the club out of the league doldrums that season or the next.

Rush's appointment as captain of the squad in the summer of 1993 seemed to galvanise the team. He also achieved a landmark 300 goals, and although far from getting back to the top of the league, the Reds landed on eighth spot.

But they did manage to bag the 1995 League Cup against Bolton Wanderers at the end of the last season in which he would make 42 appearances for the Merseyside club. Uncharacteristically, he missed a chance of a goal in the final, with his left foot, which he would normally have thumped in. Perhaps that gave fans an inkling that the end was in sight for Rush. And so it proved when Stan Collymore was brought in to boost Liverpool's striking power.

Season 1995-96 started with Rush as the chosen striker, but he was unable to score in the league until October when he bagged a brace against Manchester City. Classic Rush, he lurked in front of goal in his favourite space to pop in the rebound with his trademark coolness. He was back in a gap for another rebound, which he pounded in past the hapless keeper. But manager Roy Evans had already made decisions in his head, and Rush's place was taken by Robbie Fowler. By January of 1996, Rush had not played in the first team for two months.

Rush appeared for the last time in May 1996 in a game against Manchester City — after nine matches as a substitute — and scored the second goal in a 2-2 draw. Alert and in his favourite empty space, Rush's drive was deflected in for his final goal and the end of his Liverpool career.

Ian Rush was given the reward of a free transfer for his outstanding contribution to the club's golden era. He had scored 346 goals in his 660 games over 15 seasons. He had claimed 14 major honours, which included five league championships, the European Cup twice and the FA Cup three times. He had been nominated Liverpool top goalscorer eight times and taken home PFA, FWA and BBC awards as well as the BBC Wales Sports Personality of the Year in 1984.

On 20 May as the club entered an extended silverware drought, Rush left for Leeds United.

◄ Steve McManaman (left), Ian Rush (centre) and Dean Saunders (right) of Liverpool celebrate after their victory in the 1992 FA Cup Final against Sunderland at Wembley

▼ Liverpool celebrate their win against Sunderland with the FA Cup trophy

MOHAMED SALAH

SALAH

AN EGYPTIAN MAESTRO WHOSE BREATH-TAKING FOOTBALL SKILLS LEAVE FANS SPELLBOUND

Mohamed Salah, nicknamed "The Pharaoh" by fans and press, was born in Egypt on 15 June 1992 and joined Liverpool in 2017 after a seven-year career of increasing success, and he immediately made his presence known with goals in the Audi Cup, the Asia Trophy, two pre-season friendlies and two of the first three league games on his way to becoming top goalscorer.

◄ Mohamed Salah celebrates with Jordan Henderson after scoring the opening goal against Tottenham, 1 June 2019

▶ Mohamed Salah runs with the ball during the UEFA Champions League round of 16 second leg match between Liverpool FC and Atletico Madrid at Anfield on 11 March 2020

305 APPEARANCES

186 GOALS*

* At time of printing

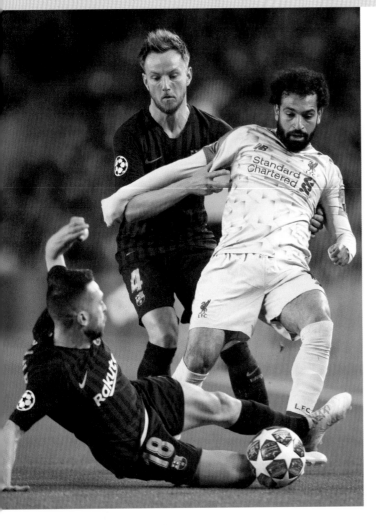

◀ Jordi Alba of Barcelona and Ivan Rakitic battle for possession with Mohamed Salah, during the UEFA Champions League semi-final first leg match, at the Nou Camp on 1 May 2019

The "Egyptian Messi" arrived at Anfield as both the BBC and CAF African Football of the Year as well as Arab Player of the Year. Having been crowned Player of the Month by supporters in August, Liverpool's first Egyptian player continued putting away goals regularly, scoring two back-to-back braces against West Ham United and Southampton while proving his credentials as a fair player by refusing to celebrate when he scored against his former club Chelsea. Salah sealed his status in the club's history by immediately turning in stunning performances claiming top goalscorer spot in 2018, aiding Liverpool's gradual rise back to silverware with a career-best tally of 44 goals, second highest in the club's history.

Salah's contribution was second to none that first season and his two unusually easy misses and an offside goal only emphasised the danger of his presence in front of goal, which he highlighted with his first goal when his split-second decision to turn a cross into a drive through the defenders and into the net, completely outwitted the opposition. Salah's speed was never more evident than when he simply left his opponents behind to power down half the field to take the return pass and when crowded down with three opposition players had the coolness to simply chip it gently past the keeper and into the net again.

One of his most memorable goals came against Watford in March 2018, a goal that made everyone aware of how good he was in a match in which he combined his swiftness, speed of thought, ball control and accurate strikes at the goal — four to be precise, beating three defenders and the keeper for his first, out-thinking them for the second, out-tricking them for the third and his lurking paying off as he belted in a rebound for his fourth. Mohammed Salah at the peak of his powers.

For his efforts, Salah was voted the PFA player of the year, the Football Writers' Footballer of the Year and Premier League Player of the Year, adding the Premier League Golden Boot for good measure.

Standing 5' 9'' tall with speed, dribbling skills, pinpoint finishing, agility and an eye for an opportunity all coupled with his ability to create opportunities for his teammates, Salah is a hard-working player, a man with superb balance and flair, who any opposing team cannot let out of their sight for a second.

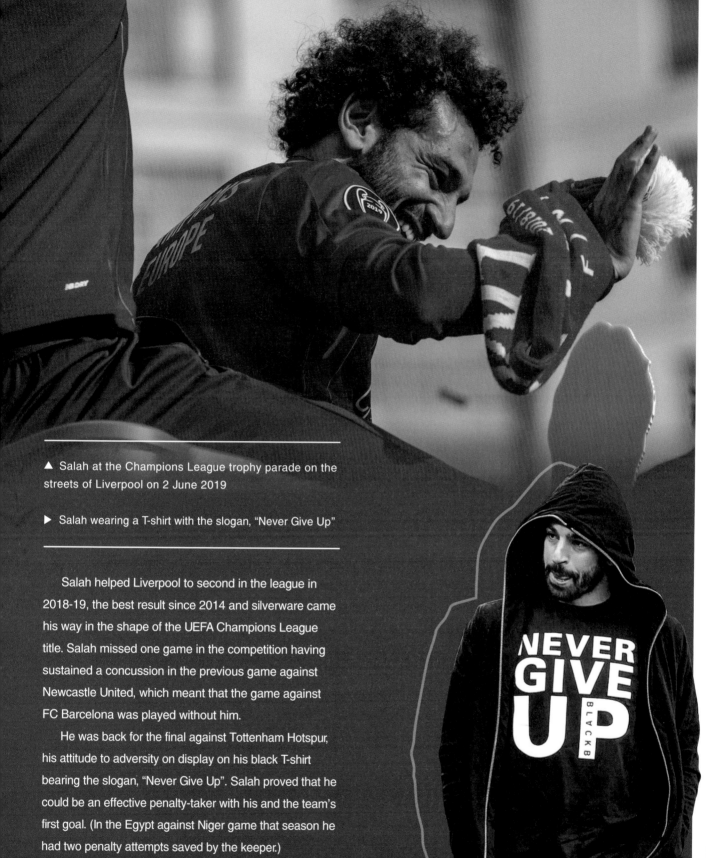

▲ Salah at the Champions League trophy parade on the streets of Liverpool on 2 June 2019

▶ Salah wearing a T-shirt with the slogan, "Never Give Up"

Salah helped Liverpool to second in the league in 2018-19, the best result since 2014 and silverware came his way in the shape of the UEFA Champions League title. Salah missed one game in the competition having sustained a concussion in the previous game against Newcastle United, which meant that the game against FC Barcelona was played without him.

He was back for the final against Tottenham Hotspur, his attitude to adversity on display on his black T-shirt bearing the slogan, "Never Give Up". Salah proved that he could be an effective penalty-taker with his and the team's first goal. (In the Egypt against Niger game that season he had two penalty attempts saved by the keeper.)

THE "EGYPTIAN MESSI"

Nonetheless, Salah's increased status in 2019 also saw him become captain of the Egypt national team.

For his third season as top goalscorer, Salah put away 23 goals to bring the club's most successful season since 2000-01 to close. His scoring rate was instrumental in helping Liverpool set a record for the most consecutive home wins, 24, and the biggest point lead at any time, 25. They also notched up the most consecutive wins, 18, and the most home wins, 18 again. There was also a 44-match unbeaten league run for fans to cheer about. Not least, Salah's goal in the match against RB Salzburg in December 2019 — once he'd missed a handful of chances. And then, challenging a defender at high speed he surged past him, rounded the goalkeeper and still at speed and at an absurdly narrow angle to the goal, curled the ball around the right post and into the net for one of the most extraordinary goals the fans had ever seen.

A penalty from Salah, vital, as it was the sixth, gave Liverpool the 2019 UEFA Super Cup against Chelsea, although examples of his clinical finishing delighted fans in games such as the one against Southampton in the league, when he darted behind the defence, a trick he repeated for his second, the defence left helpless as he sped through and the goalkeeper unable to read him until Salah had slipped the ball past into the net: Salah unstoppable and Liverpool on the way to claiming the Premier League title.

Salah blasted in the goals in 2020-21, 31 in total, scoring his 100th in October 2020 in a 2-2 away draw against Everton, although the team was unable to lift any trophies. Yet again, his goals were masterclasses in skill and calmness under pressure. He demonstrated both in the January 2021 match against West Ham, which Liverpool won 3-1. Running into the gap in the penalty area to collect the ball, he jigged with the ball back into the crowded defence against expectations, finally letting loose a left-foot drive that curled up on its way past the lunging keeper.

His perfect positioning as he sped forward again later to exploit lax defending saw him receive, control the bounce to contain the long pass, all at high speed before quickly outwitting the keeper by choosing the narrowest angle available to him and almost flick the ball with his left foot for his second goal.

◀ Salah celebrating Liverpool's victory in the 2019 UEFA Super Cup

▼ Mohamed Salah challenges Danny Rose

Salah's humble nature was always on show when he scored a goal, displaying none of the histrionics that plague many players, instead taking quiet pleasure in the joy of his teammates, the fans and his superb achievements. His character is no doubt informed by the fact that he's a devout Muslim. Charm and refusal to be drawn into the political fray have stood him in good stead and ensured his UK popularity, as was proven when both *GQ Middle East* and *Time* magazine featured him on the covers of their publications. One of the nicknames accorded him by fans, "The Egyptian King", originated with the fans yelling out, "Mo Salah! Running down the wing. Mo Salah la-la-la-la-ah, the Egyptian King."

Another record fell to him on 24 April 2021. In a 1-1 draw with Newcastle United, he was the first Liverpool player to score 20 goals in three different Premier League campaigns.

Despite the forward achieving a second-best goal tally of 31 in the 2021-22 competitions, the team again failed to take home any trophies. Nonetheless, he provided thrills aplenty; who will ever forget his performances in the games against Manchester City and Manchester United in October 2021, when his breathtaking repertoire of skills was on display.

Salah's goal against City was sensational. He took the ball outside the area, twisted and deceived three defenders who were beside him and with immaculate ball control took on two more, outpacing them, jinked left and right and through them to once again take the narrowest of angles and make it look easy to beat the keeper and score the goal. No one could believe what they had just seen.

His hat-trick in the 5-0 victory against United brought him the honour of highest-scoring African player in the history of the Premier League. Salah was again restless, looking for the fraction of a chance, thinking faster than the five defenders nearest to him took the pass and thumped the ball into the net. He waited patiently in a huge space he'd found, struck the ball first time and claimed his second. He then took off from the halfway line gathered up a beautiful pass at speed, daringly took it to within feet of the keeper before wrong-footing him and taking the narrowest angle to slot in his third as the defenders streamed in behind him.

United were walloped again in April 2022, 4-0, when Salah put another two past them and his first was the result of his quick understanding and movement as he took control of a beautiful chip while still running and with the second touch placed the ball, still pressured by defenders, into the least-expected corner of the goal.

For number two, reading the game perfectly and making sure he was well-positioned, he accelerated into the penalty area followed by just one defender to chip

▲ Murals representing Salah in (left to right);
Liverpool, Cairo and New York

▶ Mohamed Salah playing against RB Leipzig in 2022

the ball over the keeper as though he was practising alone: speed, intelligence, unflappable.

The following season saw him as sharp and quick-witted as ever taking the sliver of chance to score however the ball reached him with his trademark chips, drives, forever faster than the defenders, forever inventive, the consummate striker.

Salah has used his financial rewards to help the impoverished in his home country.

Along with a long list of personal awards, Salah's Liverpool club trophy haul includes the Premier League, FA Cup, EFL Cup, FA Community Shield, UEFA Champions League, UEFA Super Cup and FIFA Club World Cup.

TOP 50 LFC PLAYERS OF ALL TIME

Liverpool's wealth of talented players cannot be contained within a top 50 list that can only be subjective. Yet there are some names that simply stand out above all others, players of the calibre of Kenny Dalglish, Ian Rush, Kevin Keegan or Michael Owen. These players have left indelible legacies at Anfield that are beyond any doubt, as they were pivotal in ensuring the club's domestic and international successes, be it through their goalscoring exploits, technical brilliance or defensive tenacity.

▶ A selection of the greatest Liverpool players of all time

50 ❯ STEVE NICOL

Scot Steve Nicol played for Liverpool from 1981 to 1994. His versatility saw the right-back deployed in several positions; defender, midfielder, even striker on occasion. His was a crucial contribution to Liverpool's success in the 1980s and he was also capped for Scotland. Known for his excellent defending skills, his tenacity and versatility, Nicol wore the red shirt during the successful 1980s and was part of the teams that won three FA Cups and the European Cup. He put away 46 goals in 468 games for the Reds.

48 ❯ STEVE MCMANAMAN

In Steve McManaman's 365 games for Liverpool, the midfielder controlled the left-hand side of the field and was a vital cog in the team that won one League Cup, one UEFA Cup and two FA Cups. As Liverpool Player of the Year twice, McManaman scored 66 goals in the period from 1990 to 1999. He was highly valued for his speed on and off the ball, as well as his skill in creating opportunities for teammates, in tandem with his dribbling abilities.

49 ❯ XABI ALONSO

Xabi Alonso played for Liverpool as a central midfielder from 2004 to 2009. His vision and ability to control the tempo of the game combined with his passing skills saw Alonso take a vital role in Liverpool's success when he and the team won the UEFA Champions League in 2005 and the FA Cup in 2006. Alonso was Liverpool's Player of the Year in 2009. With 19 goals in total, the Spanish player appeared in 210 games for the Merseyside club.

47 ❯ JAMES MILNER

James Milner joined Liverpool in 2015. His flexibility has meant that he can play in several positions and has been seen deployed as a winger, midfielder and even a full-back. While with the club, Milner won the UEFA Champions League in 2019 and the Premier League in 2020. With a work ethic that is second to none, leadership skills and excellent crossing abilities, his main role is as a wide midfielder creating chances to score. Milner is called upon for set pieces and often used for corners and free-kicks.

46 TOMMY LAWRENCE

Scottish goalkeeper Tommy Lawrence played for Liverpool from 1957 to 1971. His agility, bravery, and excellent shot-stopping skills were priceless. His appearance between the posts during the 1960s was crucial in Liverpool's success, helping the team win two league titles, an FA Cup and a UEFA Cup. In 1963, he was named Liverpool's Player of the Year and was on the field 390 times in the red shirt. Boasting 133 clean sheets, his ability to dive around the penalty area, despite weighing more than 89 kg, earned him the affectionate nickname "The Flying Pig".

45 ALBERT STUBBINS

Englishman Albert Stubbins joined the club in 1946 and remained with them until 1953. A centre-forward known for his speed, strength and excellent finishing ability, Stubbins was essential to Liverpool's success during the 1940s. With them, he won two league titles and an FA Cup, becoming Liverpool's Player of the Year in 1947. Stubbins played a total of 178 games for Liverpool, putting away 83 goals.

44 JOHN ALDRIDGE

Widely regarded as one of the greatest Liverpool strikers of all time. The Irishman was a prolific scorer during his time at Anfield, netting 63 goals (50 in the league) in just 104 appearances between 1987 and 1989. John Aldridge's sharp finishing and poacher's instincts made him a nightmare for opposing defenders, and he was a central member of the team in Liverpool's 1987-88 league title triumph. Aldridge is remembered fondly by Liverpool fans as a true goalscoring great.

43 FERNANDO TORRES

The Spanish striker joined Liverpool in 2007, rapidly establishing himself as one of the most lethal attackers in the Premier League. With a combination of speed, skill and power that made him a huge problem for defenders to deal with, 6' 1" Fernando Torres scored an impressive 81 goals in 142 appearances for the club. One of his most memorable games came in the 2008-09 season, when he scored a stunning header and a punt past the keeper in a 2-0 win against Chelsea.

42 ❯ GERRY BYRNE

Not be a name that younger Liverpool fans will know, left-back Gerry Byrne spent his entire career at Liverpool in both the youth and senior teams. With 333 senior appearances and four goals for Liverpool between 1957 and 1964, he was the rock at the back of the team that won two league titles, an FA Cup, and a European Cup during that period. Never a flashy player, he was known as a tenacious defender, who would not shy away from tough tackling and Byrne possessed an excellent positional sense.

41 ❯ STEVE MCMAHON

Midfielder Steve McMahon arrived at the club in 1985 and stayed with the club until 1991 having made 277 appearances and scored 50 goals in total. He soon made himself a fans' favourite with his no-nonsense tackling — which sometimes veered over into outright aggression — and his superb technical abilities. He was a frequent goalscorer, four times during a famous 10-0 victory against Fulham and went on to win the league three times with Liverpool, donning the captain's armband in the 1989-90 campaign. He was capped for England 17 times.

40 ❯ JIMMY CASE

Midfielder Jimmy Case played for the club from 1975 to 1981. He was a versatile player who played both in defence and midfield and was known for his powerful shooting, tenacity and determination. Spectacular goals came from his boot — such as the two he scored when he wreaked havoc in the European Cup semi-final of 1977 as Liverpool beat FC Zürich 3-0, the first coming when he pounced in the penalty area to rob the defender and place the ball in the net and the second was a ferocious free-kick from outside the box.

39 ❯ MICHAEL OWEN

Hard-working Michael Owen was a striker who possessed incredible speed and a sizzling finish, with score ratio of one goal every two games for Liverpool. He played for the club from 1996 to 2004 and his playing style was characterised by his ability to get in behind defences and his speed. His stunning goal in the 2001 FA Cup final — after he had darted into a crowd of defenders to slide-kick the ball into the net for his first — when he hurtled down the pitch, shook off the defenders and sliced the ball across the keeper for his second and the winning goal was an Owen classic.

38 › SAMMY LEE

Playing for the club from 1976 to 1986 in 295 games, Sammy Lee's style was distinguished by his energy, and despite his diminutive size, he was 5' 4" tall, a willingness to put his physique on the line for the team. Accurate passing ability in tandem with his high work rate and ability to break up opposition playing midfield helped him to control the midfield area. He was on target eight times in the 1980-81 season, the first in which he played a full season of games.

37 › JOHN TOSHACK

John Toshack was a dominant force in the air, his height and strength making him a tough opponent for defenders to overcome. His ability to score goals helped Liverpool to many successes, and his strength on the ball and his height — his talent never more in evidence than during the Charity Shield match of 1976, when he left defenders floundering to blast a shot into the net — were invaluable assets. His partnership with Kevin Keegan enabled him to win two league titles, the European Cup, the FA Cup and two UEFA Cups over eight years with the Reds.

36 › ROBERTO FIRMINO

A creative player who is comfortable dropping deep to receive the ball as an attacking midfielder and create space for his teammates, Roberto Firmino joined the club in 2015 and his talents enable him to play in multiple positions from where he can be directly involved in making opportunities for his teammates. The forward is a powerful striker of the ball as he proved in the 2017-18 season with 27 goals in all competitions including two in the 5-2 victory against AS Roma in a UEFA Champions League match. Jürgen Klopp described him as the engine of the team.

35 JAN MØLBY

Danish midfielder Jan Mølby was known for his passing ability and calmness under pressure, which enabled him to score a vital penalty against Liverpool in 1986. The 6' 2" Danish international played for Liverpool from 1984 until 1996 as a deep-lying playmaker who could dictate play from midfield. His playing style was characterised by composure on the ball, and an ability to control the tempo of the game. He was a prolific penalty-taker scoring 42 for the club missing just three.

33 BRUCE GROBBELAAR

Bruce Grobbelaar played for Liverpool from 1981 until 1994 claiming 267 clean sheets. Born in Zimbabwe, he was an eccentric player who was willing to take risks, but his unorthodox style, especially his agility and his shotstopping ability were vital to the Liverpool team. His acrobatic saves and ability to rise to the occasion at crucial moments were seen at their best in the 1984 European Cup final, when he held off Roma brilliantly. Who can forget his wobbly-leg routine as he saved two penalties in the shoot-out to help Liverpool to their fourth European Cup victory.

34 JORDAN HENDERSON

A hard-working player who is known for his leadership qualities both on and off the field, his playing style is notable for ability to cover ground and his accurate passing. Jordan Henderson joined Liverpool in 2011 and is known as a box-to-box midfielder but can take up many positions in midfield. His ability to strike powerful goals was valuable during 480 games yielding 33 goals, although his first goal of the 2019 season arrived when he came roaring in to put away the third goal in a 3-1 victory.

32 TRENT ALEXANDER-ARNOLD

The English right-back emerged from the Liverpool youth squad as one of Liverpool's best players. Known for his attacking ability, his crossing and his set-piece delivery, he also possesses an ability to get forward and provide width for the Liverpool attack. In defence, his solid performances and positional sense have been invaluable. Neither is he afraid to go forward and score goals, something he proved in the 2019-20 Premier League when his daring runs up front produced four goals.

31 ⟩ RONNIE WHELAN

Irish midfielder Ronnie Whelan was a Liverpool player from 1979 to 1994. He combined his ability to score goals with versatility and technical skill and was valued for his work rate and adaptability in taking over various multiple midfield positions. One of his goals, considered among the best in League Cup history, came with an extraordinary long curling strike in the 1983 League Cup final against Manchester United. In his 493 appearances for the club he scored 73 goals.

30 ⟩ RAY KENNEDY

A player with many facets, Ray Kennedy was an essential member of Liverpool's success in the late 1970s and early 1980s. In 393 appearances for the club and scoring 72 goals, Kennedy could play anywhere across the midfield or as a striker. Valued for his powerful runs, excellent dribbling skills and ability to score goals from midfield, Kennedy was, according to Bob Paisley: "…one of Liverpool's greatest players and probably the most underrated".

29 ⟩ ANDY ROBERTSON

Left-back Andy Robertson has established himself as one of the best defenders in the world since joining Liverpool in 2017. Never afraid to go forward when he can also score goals, one of his best arriving in a dramatic match against Red Bull Salzburg when Robertson timed his run-in perfectly to score his first European goal and help seal a dramatic 4-3 victory. Known for his incredible work rate, crossing ability and defensive solidity, Robertson's playing style is based around his ability to overlap and provide support to his team's attacks while also being a defensive hard-man.

28 ⟩ MARK LAWRENSON

Solid as a rock in the Liverpool defence during the 1980s, Mark Lawrenson turned in 356 appearances for the club and scored 18 goals. Lawrenson was a composed defender who could play in the centre or on the right. He was known for his excellent tackling, reading of the game, and composure under pressure and Lawrenson's intelligent understanding of game play helped him to make crucial interceptions and tackles to block the opposition's attacks.

26 ⟩ RAY CLEMENCE

Liverpool goalkeeper in the 1970s and early 1980s, Ray Clemence was between the sticks for the Reds 665 times and he kept 323 clean sheets in his career with the Reds, a club record. Clemence was a commanding presence in the box and was known for his excellent shot-stopping ability. His best moment came in the 1977 European Cup final against Borussia Mönchengladbach, where he made a crucial save to deny Mönchengladbach's Allan Simonsen a goal. Clemence was noted for his ability to organise his defence and for his excellent understanding of ball distribution.

27 ⟩ TERRY MCDERMOTT

A clever midfielder for Liverpool in the 1970s and 1980s, Terry McDermott made 329 appearances for the club. McDermott was known for his powerful shots from distance and his ability to score crucial goals, and his final tally for the club was 81. One his best came in the 1977 European Cup final against Borussia Mönchengladbach, where he scored a beautifully placed goal to help Liverpool win their first European Cup. McDermott's owes his success to his high energy, aggressive pressing and his ability to contribute to both attacking and defensive phases of play.

25 ⟩ ALAN KENNEDY

Alan Kennedy played for Liverpool in the late 1970s and early 1980s in the left-back position. With 359 appearances for the club and 20 goals, Kennedy was known for his pace and his excellent crossing ability. The best goal of his career was scored in the 1981 European Cup final against Real Madrid, where he scored the winning goal by pouncing on a half-chance, with courage and a superb finish. Kennedy's game was renowned for his overlapping runs down the left flank and his ability to provide excellent crosses into the box for his teammates.

Alisson arrived in Liverpool in 2018, and has been a vital part of their success since then. He has now made over 162 appearances for the club and has been awarded the Yashin Trophy. His superb shot-stopping ability and his excellent distribution skills have made him a favourite with fans and he is considered one of the best goalkeepers in the world. His skills were again on show in the 2022 UEFA Champions League match against Benfica, where he made a stunning save to prevent Darwin Núñez's powerful effort from hitting the bottom corner of the net. Alisson's game plan is based on his ability to command his area and his awareness of his teammates' positions, enabling him to assist Liverpool in launching quick counter-attacks from the back.

23 > TOMMY SMITH

Darling of the Kop and superb defender Tommy Smith, who spent nearly his entire career at Liverpool from 1962 to 1978, made 638 appearances for the club and scored 48 goals. Renowned for his tough-tackling style and his ability to score crucial goals from set-pieces, perhaps his crowning moment was during the 1977 European Cup final against Borussia Mönchengladbach. With a thunderous header he ensured that Liverpool took the lead and would win the tie. Smith's style was formed around his physicality and his ability to read the game, which allowed him to make crucial interceptions and tackles in key areas of the pitch.

22 > SAMI HYYPIÄ

Centre-back Sami Hyypiä was a distinguished captain of the club until Steven Gerrard took over, playing from 1999 and making 464 appearances over 10 years. A crucial member of Liverpool's defence during his tenure at the club, the Finnish international netted 35 goals in the process. His standout moments were the three goals he scored in the Champions League quarter-finals, the first in 2002 against Leverkusen, then in 2005 against Juventus and against Arsenal in 2008. Known for his towering presence, aerial prowess, and ability to lead his teammates, Hyypiä was also an astute reader of the game, and his passing range was a valuable asset to Liverpool's attacking play.

21 ❯ STEVE HEIGHWAY

Irishman Steve Heighway's exciting play on the wing was seen between 1970 and 1981, when he made 475 appearances and scored 76 goals. One of his best goals came in the 1971 FA Cup final against Arsenal, when he scythed down the pitch and dribbled past several defenders before slotting the ball into the net from a narrow angle. His pace, skill and creativity paired with his ability to create chances for his teammates was instrumental in Liverpool's success during the 1970s. He remains a beloved figure among Liverpool fans and is considered one of the greatest wingers in the club's history.

20 ❯ RON YEATS

Centre-half Ron Yeats was a legendary Liverpool player who made 454 appearances for the club between 1961 and 1971 scoring 16 goals. He was known for his commanding presence on the pitch and his ability to read the game. A formidable defender, Yeats was indisputably key to Liverpool's success during the 1960s, which included winning the league championship twice. With his towering frame and no-nonsense playing style Yeats was a fan favourite at Anfield, and he was also the team captain for several years, a beloved figure in Liverpool's history. He said of himself: "I was a tackler, a header of the ball and read the game well. I got the ball and gave it to someone who could pass it. I knew my limitations. I was very left-footed."

19 ❯ PHIL THOMPSON

Phil Thompson is a Liverpool idol having played for the club for 13 years from 1971 to 1984. The centre-back made 477 appearances for the Reds and was feared by opposition teams for his tough-tackling defensive style, which made him a central force in the Liverpool teams in the 1970s and early 1980s. Also valued for his leadership skills, he was captain of the team for a period of time. He could also score goals such as the one he headed in during the 2-0 league defeat of Sunderland in 1977. One of the most decorated players in the history of English football, Thompson was affectionately known as "Thommo" by Liverpool fans.

18 ❯ JAMIE CARRAGHER

One of Liverpool's most iconic defenders, Jamie Carragher played for the club for 17 years from 1996 to 2013 making 737 appearances for the Reds and scored five goals. A defence without Carragher's no-nonsense defending style was unthinkable for the Liverpool teams of the 2000s with whom he won multiple trophies including the Champions League in 2005, the FA Cup twice and the League Cup three times. He was also known for his versatility, having played in both centre-back and full-back positions throughout his career. He was affectionately known as "Carra" by Liverpool fans.

17 ROBBIE FOWLER

During his two spells at the club totalling eight years from 1993 to 2001 and 2006 to 2007, Robbie Fowler became one of Liverpool's most prolific strikers. He made 369 appearances for the Reds and scored 183 goals. Fowler was known for his deadly finishing ability and was a fan favourite at Anfield, where he was affectionately known as "God" by Liverpool fans. As a crucial part of Liverpool's successful teams in the 1990s, Fowler won multiple trophies including the FA Cup and League Cup. One his most exhilarating matches for Liverpool came in the league against Middlesbrough in 1995 when he put away four goals.

16 SADIO MANÉ

Sadio Mané counts among Liverpool's most exciting attackers, playing for the club from 2016 until 2022, clocking up 260 appearances for the Reds with 120 goals. Mané's lightning-fast pace and excellent dribbling skills paired with his unpredictability made him a constant threat to opposition defences. His style was mesmerising and he won the Champions League in 2019 and the Premier League in 2020. A typical Mané goal for Liverpool came in a Premier League match against Arsenal in 2018, when he scored by speeding past defenders to take a pass, judge the ball's bounce in a split-second and volley the ball into the back of the net. He is affectionately known as "Sadio" by Liverpool fans.

15 EMLYN HUGHES

Emlyn Hughes was in red for 12 years from 1967 to 1979. In 474 league appearances he scored 35 goals. A commanding presence on the pitch, his tough-tackling defending cemented the defence of Liverpool's successful teams in the 1970s, when Hughes won multiple trophies including the European Cup in 1977 and 1978. In a league match against Ipswich, Hughes showed what he was capable of with an absolute scorcher shot from outside the box into the net, a highlight for him in his Liverpool career. He was affectionately known as "Crazy Horse" by Liverpool fans.

Playing for the club for 10 years from 1961 to 1971, Ian St John made 425 appearances for the Reds and scored 118 goals. The forward's clinical finishing ability and his excellent movement off the ball made him a vital element in the Liverpool teams of the 1960s, and he helped the club win its first ever FA Cup in 1965. St John will always be remembered, but especially for his most crucial goal, which came in the 1965 FA Cup final when he flew through the air in a dive to head the ball past the Leeds United goalkeeper and win the match. He was nicknamed "The Saint".

In an all-time record 857 appearances Ian Callaghan scored 68 goals, at least one in all but three seasons between 1959 and 1978. Callaghan's tireless work rate in midfield made him an indispensable member of the Liverpool teams in the 1960s and 1970s, when he won many trophies, one of which was the European Cup in 1977. His versatility ensured that he was able to play in both midfield and defensive positions throughout his career. Callaghan was on target 10 times in the 1968-69 season, a career best, scoring the goal that won the match on more than one occasion. The Liverpool faithful knew him simply as "Cally".

Playfully known as "Jock" by Liverpool fans, Alan Hansen was noticeable for his elegant playing style and was a key member of Liverpool's successful teams in the 1980s, winning multiple trophies including the European Cup three times. Having played for the club in 620 games in 14 years from 1977 to 1991, the centre-back was also greatly valued for his leadership skills and was given the captaincy. He scored 14 goals, and formed an "almost telepathic" duo with Thompson, although his tackling skills were the subject of mild humour among pundits.

Billy Liddell is a true Liverpool legend who thrilled fans for 23 years from 1938 until 1961. He played in 534 games and scored 228 goals. Liddell's pace and dribbling skills ensured that he was a kingpin for Liverpool's teams of the 1940s and 1950s, when he helped them take home the First Division title in 1947. His loyalty to the club saw him turn down offers from other top teams. Liverpool's brightest star, Liddell was the club's top scorer seven times. "He was fast, powerful, shot with either foot and his headers were like blasts from a gun. On top of all that he was as hard as granite," was Bill Shankly's enthusiastic opinion of Liddell. He will always be remembered as "Mr Liddellpool" among the Liverpool fans.

Kevin Keegan played for Liverpool for six years between 1971 and 1977, making 323 appearances and scoring 100 goals. A hard-working and versatile player displaying a good work ethic and superb skills, Keegan was also known for his tireless running. With excellent dribbling skills and an eye for an opportunity, among his many memorable goals for the club, were those in the FA Cup final against Newcastle United in 1974, when he flicked the ball up to volley in his first and found yards of space to tap in his second. Keegan was affectionately referred to as "Super Kev".

9 ▸ GRAEME SOUNESS

Playing in red for six years between 1978 and 1984, making 359 appearances and scoring 55 goals, Graeme Souness was a tough-tackling midfielder, whose value was also apparent in his leadership qualities. The 5' 11" Scot was a vital linchpin in Liverpool's 1980s successes and contributed a number of important goals for the club, putting away 13 in the 1980-81 season. Souness was a highly respected member of the team, known by his nickname "Souey", one of the best midfielders of his generation.

Appearing in 492 matches and scoring 285 goals in all competitions, Roger Hunt played for Liverpool between 1959 and 1969. One of the club's greatest-ever players, his precision finishing made him a feared member of the 1960s team, his combination of pace, skill and power making him a nightmare for defenders to handle. He paired intelligent movement around the field with his uncanny ability to be in the right place at the right time. Top goalscorer on nine occasions, he put away a career best 32 in the 1965-66 season hitting a famous hat-trick against Sunderland in 1966. One of his best goals was his thunderous drive for his second in that game. He was respectfully referred to as "Sir Roger".

7 ▶ VIRGIL VAN DIJK

The Dutch centre-back joined the club in 2018 and has since built a reputation as one of the world's best defenders. With his exceptional defensive skills, including his strong aerial ability, strength, and tackling, the centre-back is also a leader on the field, commanding the backline and helping to organise the defence. Van Dijk also roams forward to score, netting six in the 2018-19 season when his first Premier League goal came from a volley after Mohamed Salah's cross, ensuring Liverpool's 2-1 victory. His skill and playing style have earned him the nickname "The Rolls Royce of defenders", and he was a solid presence in Liverpool's successful 2018-19 season

6 ▶ IAN RUSH, OBE

Welsh striker Ian Rush played for Liverpool from 1980 until 1986 and again from 1988 to 1996. He played over 660 games and scored a total of 346 goals. He is renowned as the best goalscorer in the club's history. In 1983 he slotted five past the Luton side as part of the team that was dubbed "The greatest team in the country". His skill and playing style earned him the nickname "Rushie", and he remains a beloved figure among Liverpool fans. Rush was known for his razor-sharp finishing, his speed, and his ability to create scoring opportunities for himself and his teammates. He was a natural goalscorer, who instinctively knew the best positions from which to reach the back of the net.

5 ▶ JOHN BARNES

With 407 appearances for the club in which he scored a total of 108 goals, the former England left-winger played for Liverpool from 1987 to 1997. Barnes was known for his incredible skill on the ball, his vision, and fearlessly taking on multiple defenders at once. He was a creative force in Liverpool's midfield, providing assists and scoring goals, and his greatest performance came on 17 October 1987 against Queens Park Rangers. He scored what he considers the best goal of his career, charging down the field with the ball to dodge around three defenders. His skill and playing style earned him the nickname "Digger", and he is still one of Liverpool FC's most iconic players.

4 ▶ LUIS SUÁREZ

In 133 appearances, the Uruguayan striker scored 82 goals at the club. Luis Suárez's playing style was characterised by his incredible dribbling skills, pace and precision finishing ability, earning him the nickname "El Pistolero" or "The Gunman". He was a master of creating space for himself and his teammates and was never afraid to take on defenders one-on-one. Suárez's outstanding talent made him one of the most influential players in Liverpool's recent history and he will always be remembered for his four-goal blitz of Norwich City on 4 December 2013 when Liverpool handed out a 5-1 drubbing.

3 ▶ MOHAMED SALAH

Mohamed Salah joined the club in 2017, ended his first season with the Reds with a career-best 44 goals and has topped the goalscoring table in every season since. Salah's playing style is characterised by his incredible pace, lightness on his feet, dribbling skills and finishing skill and accuracy. Nicknamed "The Egyptian King" by Liverpool fans due to his outstanding performances and incredible goalscoring record, Salah's ability to create chances and score goals has made him one of Liverpool's most important players in recent years. Salah surpassed Robbie Fowler as Premier League top goalscorer for Liverpool.

2 ▶ STEVEN GERRARD

Joining the club in 1998, Steven Gerrard made 710 appearances for the club, scoring 186 goals. Nicknamed "Stevie G" by Liverpool fans and one of the most iconic players in the club's history, Gerrard's outstanding playing ability and leadership skills earned him a regular place in Liverpool's teams during his time at the club. His incredible long-range strike against West Ham United in the 2006 FA Cup final was an example of his powerful shooting and eye for a chance. Gerrard was known for the varied range of his passes, his leadership on the pitch, and his ability to score important goals.

1 ▶ KENNY DALGLISH

Liverpool favourite Kenny Dalglish made 515 appearances for the club and netted 172 goals in total between the years of 1977 to 1990 (as player-manager from 1985). Dalglish's playing style was distinguished by his incredible dribbling skills, vision, and clinical finishing ability, earning him the nickname "King Kenny" among Liverpool fans. He scored in every season except his last three (with just three appearances as player-manager) with a career best of 31 on his Liverpool debut. He was a master at creating chances for himself and his teammates and was known for his ability to dictate the pace of the game. Dalglish's outstanding playing ability and leadership skills earned him the captaincy and made him one of the greatest footballers ever to play at Liverpool, an indispensable member of the club's successful teams.

THE GREATEST LFC MANAGERS OF ALL TIME

Liverpool FC's greatest managers have left an indelible mark on the club and the sport of football. Their passion, dedication and unwavering commitment to excellence have led to some of the most memorable moments in the club's history. Their ability to motivate and inspire their players, coupled with their tactical genius, have helped to shape the club into the formidable force it is today. Their legacies will continue to be celebrated by fans for generations to come.

▶ The Boot Room Boys (from left to right) Liverpool manager Bill Shankly poses with his coaching staff known as 'Liverpool Boot Room' Bob Paisley, Ronnie Moran, Joe Fagan and Reuben Bennett during a photoshoot held in the 1960s at Anfield

BILL SHANKLY

A MASTER MOTIVATOR WITH A DEEP UNDERSTANDING OF HIS PLAYERS

Born on 2 September 1913, Bill Shankly is a name synonymous with Liverpool Football Club. Widely regarded as one of the greatest football managers of all time, he is credited with turning Liverpool into the powerhouse they are today. Shankly managed Liverpool for 15 years, from 1959 to 1974, during which time he oversaw 783 games, winning 407 of them.

Liverpool were languishing in the Second Division when he arrived, and he began to put together a team that would become one of the best in the First Division.

During his most successful seasons in the mid-1960s and early 1970s, Liverpool won two league titles, two FA Cups and the UEFA Cup. Shankly founded his teams' successes on a strong defence and a tireless work ethic, introducing the "boot-room" philosophy, where coaches and players would gather to discuss tactics and strategy.

Many factors conjoined to make Shankly the exceptional manager that he was. Clear vision and a strong personality were key factors, but he was also a master motivator with a deep understanding of his players' strengths and weaknesses. He was also an astute tactician who was able to devise game plans that would exploit his opponents' weaknesses. Shankly was also a great communicator, his enthusiasm prompting his players to give their all for the club.

Shankly mentored several players to success during his time at Liverpool. Among those who benefitted from his guidance and coaching was Ian St John, a talented striker who Shankly helped develop into one of the best forwards in the game. And, of course, Kevin Keegan, the talented young striker who Shankly helped develop into a world-class player. Shankly favoured hard-working players who were willing to put the team first. He encouraged players to be aggressive and physical on the pitch, but also emphasised the importance of skill and technique.

Among a welter of exciting games, these three of Shankly's can be counted as outstanding: the 1965 FA Cup final: Liverpool vs. Leeds United. This was Shankly's first major trophy as Liverpool manager, and his team won a tense match 2-1 after extra-time. Liverpool's first came from a Roger Hunt header and the winner came from another header, this time by Ian St John. The 1973 UEFA Cup final: Liverpool vs. Borussia Mönchengladbach. Liverpool gained their first European trophy under Shankly's management in this final, 3-2 on aggregate after a thrilling second leg. The first leg, played at Anfield, was particularly memorable, with Liverpool winning 3-0. The 1974 FA Cup final: Liverpool vs. Newcastle. This proved to be Shankly's last major trophy as Liverpool manager, and it was won in magnificent fashion 3-0 thanks to a brace of goals by

Keegan and a Heighway third goal.

Shankly enjoyed his most successful seasons with the 1963-64 and 1972-73 campaigns. In 1963-64, Liverpool won the league title for the first time in 17 years, with Roger Hunt finishing as the league's top scorer. In 1972-73, Liverpool won the league title and the UEFA Cup, with Kevin Keegan and John Toshack forming a deadly strike partnership.

Away from football, Shankly was known for his commitment to the Liverpool community. He was a socialist who believed in the power of football to bring people together and saw Liverpool Football Club as a way of giving hope to the working-class people of the city. Shankly was also a man of great humour and wit, and he was known for his quick one-liners and his love of a good joke.

A man who is often described as being a tough, no-nonsense character both on and off the pitch, Shankly was feared for his direct and often blunt communication style. However, he was also a very passionate and charismatic individual, who was deeply loved by Liverpool fans and players alike. He will always be revered for his famous words: "Some people believe football is a matter of life and death, I am very disappointed with that attitude. I can assure you it is much, much more important than that."

▲ Bill Shankly celebrates in front of the Liverpool fans

Bill Shankly died on 29 September 1981.

Some of the honours Bill Shankly was awarded:

Personal Awards:
▶ Inducted into the English Football Hall of Fame in 2002;
▶ Named Manager of the Year by the English Football Writers' Association in 1964, 1966 and 1973;
▶ Received the Order of the British Empire (OBE) in 1974 for services to football;
▶ Awarded Honorary Freedom of the City of Liverpool in 1975;
▶ Named Manager of the Year by the League Managers' Association in 1976;
▶ Inducted into the Scottish Football Hall of Fame in 2004

Club Awards:
▶ Football League First Division: 1963-64, 1965-66, 1972-73;
▶ Football League Second Division: 1961-62;
▶ FA Cup: 1964-65, 1973-74;
▶ FA Charity Shield: 1964, 1965, 1966;
▶ UEFA Cup: 1972-73

BOB PAISLEY

Bob Paisley was born on 23 January 1919 and took over as manager of Liverpool aged 55 when Bill Shankly retired in 1974 having joined Liverpool as a player in May 1939, and he retired from playing in 1954 after 253 appearances. Thereafter, he became a physiotherapist for the club and assistant manager from 1959 to 1974. He was one of the original members of the "boot room" initiated by Bill Shankly as a place to discuss tactics.

Widely considered to be one of the greatest managers of all time, Paisley managed Liverpool Football Club from 1974 until 1983, and during his tenure he established the club as a dominant force in English and European football.

In his nine years at the club, Paisley oversaw 535 matches, winning 308 of them. He won six league titles, three European Cups, one UEFA Cup, and three League Cups, making him the most successful manager in Liverpool's history.

His managerial talent was founded upon several factors that built on the groundwork laid by his predecessor, Bill Shankly, and which would take the team to even greater heights. He was known in particular for his calm and measured approach and his ability to get the best out of his players.

Paisley invested time in several players and helped them succeed. Three players who benefitted greatly from his guidance and coaching were Kenny Dalglish, Graeme Souness and Alan Hansen. Dalglish and Souness became key players for Liverpool during Paisley's period as manager and were instrumental in the club's success. Hansen was a talented young defender who Paisley brought into the first team and helped grow into one of the best defenders in the game.

Among Paisley's best matches, these three deserve special mention: The 1977 European Cup final, Liverpool vs. Borussia Mönchengladbach. This was Paisley's first European Cup final as Liverpool manager, and his team put in a dominant performance to win 3-1. The match marked the beginning of Liverpool's domination of European football under Paisley.

Secondly, the 1978 European Cup final, Liverpool vs. Club Brugge: this match saw Liverpool win their second European Cup under Paisley's management. They won 1-0, with Kenny Dalglish scoring the only goal of the game.

Thirdly, the 1981 European Cup final, Liverpool vs. Real Madrid: this game delivered what was arguably Paisley's greatest triumph as Liverpool manager. His team faced a formidable Real Madrid team in the final but won 1-0, with Alan Kennedy scoring the winning goal.

Among the many successful campaigns under Paisley's guidance, were the 1975-76, 1976-77 and the

1978-79 campaigns; outstanding seasons. In 1975-76, Liverpool won the First Division title and the UEFA Cup, in 1976-77 the league title and the European Cup, while in 1977-78, they won the European Cup and European Super Cup.

Off the football pitch, Paisley was known for his humble and unassuming personality. A man of few words, he preferred to let his team's performances do the talking. He was a lifelong Liverpool fan and had a deep connection with the club and its supporters.

One of the greatest football managers of any

club at any time, Bob Paisley's impact on Liverpool Football Club cannot be overstated. He led the club to unprecedented success and established them as one of the dominant forces in English and European football. Paisley's calm and measured approach and his ability to get the best out of his players were key factors in his success, and his legacy continues to inspire Liverpool fans to this day.

By the time Paisley retired in 1983 he had spent 44 years at the club. He then became a club director and right-hand man to Kenny Dalglish when Dalglish became manager.

Bob Paisley died on 14 February 1996. Paisley's legacy at Liverpool continues to inspire fans and players to this day.

Some of Paisley's most notable awards and achievements include:

Personal Awards:
▶ Named Manager of the Year by the English Football Writers' Association in 1976, 1977 and 1983;
▶ Named Manager of the Year by the League Managers' Association in 1980 and 1982;
▶ Received the Order of the British Empire (OBE) in 1977 for services to football;
▶ Inducted into the English Football Hall of Fame in 2002

Club Awards:
▶ Led Liverpool to win the First Division championship six times (in 1976, 1977, 1979, 1980, 1982 and 1983);
▶ Won the European Cup three times (in 1977, 1978 and 1981);
▶ Won the UEFA Cup once (in 1976);
▶ Won the League Cup three times (in 1981, 1982 and 1983);
▶ Won the Charity Shield six times (in 1974, 1976, 1977, 1979, 1980 and 1982);
▶ Led Liverpool to win the European Super Cup once (in 1977)

JOE FAGAN

Joe Fagan is a name that resonates with many football fans in Liverpool. The former footballer turned manager and coach played a significant role in the development of the game in the city during his tenure as a coach. Born in Liverpool in 1949, Fagan started his football career as a player in the 1960s. He played for several clubs, including Bristol Rovers, Tranmere Rovers and Port Vale, before retiring in 1978 due to injury.

Fagan became a highly successful football manager who spent the majority of his management career at Liverpool football club, joining the team, initially, to work as a coach for the club's reserve team. He went on to become assistant manager under Bob Paisley, before taking the top job himself in 1983.

"My first reaction at the time was that I wouldn't take it," he said, "but I thought about it carefully and realised someone else might come in and upset the whole rhythm. I finally decided to take it and keep the continuity going for a little longer."

During his time at Liverpool, Fagan oversaw some of the club's greatest-ever matches. His contribution as manager in what was one of Liverpool's standout performances, in the 1984 European Cup final, where Liverpool beat AS Roma on penalties 4-2 to claim their fourth European Cup cannot be overlooked — as Alan Kennedy later affirmed. It was Fagan's tactical

design, neutralising the Roma strikers, that was vital to Liverpool's victory. Fagan had instructed the Liverpool players to track the runs of Falcão, Roma's dangerous attacking midfielder.

Fagan's second season in charge was less successful and the club fell to second in the league and also failed to bring in any silverware from the FA, First Division or European competitions although they were runners-up in all three European ties.

Although he had intended to, and did, only stay as manager for two seasons, in that short time Fagan had built a team that was defensively solid and skilled at mounting quick counter-attacks. The team's fighting spirit and determination were also a credit to Fagan's positive approach to management. "His way would be a quiet word or even a single look," Graeme Souness remembered. "He could be hard and I remember on a number of occasions that he would say something really harsh to one of the lads, but he'd do it ever so quietly and that was his way of emphasising the point."

Fagan's success at Liverpool can be attributed to his excellent managerial skills. He was an unassuming and modest man greatly appreciated for his calm and measured approach, and his ability to get the best out of his players. Fagan had a deep understanding of the game, and was highly respected by his everyone. He was able to motivate and inspire his teams and was valued for his positive approach to management, his tactical knowledge and his attention to detail.

Fagan was particularly influential in the development of Ian Rush, who went on to become one of Liverpool's greatest-ever players and helped to bring through a number of other talented young players, including Mark Lawrenson and Ronnie Whelan and Ian St John.

Joe Fagan was possessed of a no-nonsense personality and a deep love for football. He was a man of few words, but when he spoke, people listened and man management was one of Fagan's strong points.

Fagan, who kept his personal life private, was married to Lillian Poke and the couple had six children. Known for his strong work ethic, he was deeply committed to his family. The events in the 1985 European Cup final when 39 Juventus fans died affected him very deeply as the photos at the time of the shattered manager returning home prove. The evening haunted him for the rest of his life.

Joe Fagan had a profound impact on Liverpool Football Club during his time there. His participation in turning Liverpool from a struggling Second Division club, together with Shankly and Paisley, has been

described as "both pioneering and undoubtedly vital" and his historic triple-winning year of 1983-84 will never be forgotten.

Joe Fagan was the recipient of several honours during his time at the club:

Personal Awards:
▶ Manager of the Year, 1984;
▶ The Freedom of the City of Liverpool, 1984;
▶ UEFA Order of Merit 1985;
▶ Fagan was inducted into the English Football Hall of Fame, 2002;
▶ Inducted into the Liverpool Hall of Fame, 2004;
▶ Order of the British Empire (OBE) 1986

Club Awards:
▶ European Cup: 1983-84;
▶ English First Division: 1983-84;
▶ English League Cup: 1983-84

▼ Joe Fagan pictured by the pool the morning after Liverpool's European Cup victory against Roma, May 1984

KENNY DALGLISH, OBE

DALGLISH

KNOWN FOR HIS WORK IN DEVELOPING YOUNG PLAYERS

Kenny Dalglish was not only one of Liverpool FC's greatest players, but also one of its most successful managers. Taking over as player-manager in 1985, he led Liverpool to three league titles and two FA Cup victories during his tenure. It is likely the man who exercised the greatest influence on his future career was Jock Stein at Celtic, renowned for his tactical acumen and emphasis on discipline and hard work. However, it is also safe to say that Dalglish developed his own management style over the years, based on his own experiences as a player and his observations of other successful managers.

One of Dalglish's most successful games must be the 1989 FA Cup final, where Liverpool defeated Everton 3-2 in a thrilling match that is still remembered as one of the greatest cup finals of all time. Dalglish's team also won the 1986 FA Cup final, in which they again defeated local rivals Everton 3-1. Dalglish's Liverpool team clinched the league title in 1988 with a 3-1 victory over West Ham United in a match that saw Liverpool score three goals in the final 15 minutes to secure the championship.

That year of 1989, Liverpool won the Championship race for the 18th time and Dalglish was handed the Manager of the Year award his third time in five years.

Dalglish was instrumental in the development of numerous Liverpool players, including Steve McManaman and Michael Owen. In addition to his success on the pitch, Dalglish is also known for his work in developing young players. Dalglish's ability to identify and nurture young talent helped to secure the future of Liverpool FC, and his contributions to the club's youth system are still evident today.

Dalglish's success as a manager was due in large part to his excellent coaching skills. When he first took over the hot seat he made immediate changes to stamp his mark on the team replacing the full-backs of the Paisley era, Phil Neal and Alan Kennedy, using Steve Nicol and Jim Beglin instead. Dalglish also introduced a sweeper role into the team, which altered the team's playing style when 6' 2" Dane Jan Mølby was cast in that role. His teams played more offensive football than those of his predecessors and his style owed more to the individual play of great players while maintaining a high team spirit.

Known for his attention to detail and his ability to motivate his players, Dalglish was highly respected by his peers in the football world. His tactical acumen was second to none and he was a master in assembling teams that were both defensively solid making them notoriously difficult to score against and dangerous on the attack. With a keen eye for talent, Dalglish was responsible for nurturing some of the greatest player's in Liverpool's history. The names of such players are still revered today,

▲ Ronnie Moran, Kenny Dalglish and Roy Evans celebrate the Championship win with the trophies, 1 May 1990

men such as John Barnes or John Aldridge, one of the most prolific goalscorers in Liverpool's history.

With meticulous preparation and willing to adjust his tactics to suit the strengths and weaknesses of his opponents, Kenny Dalglish was famous for his ability to motivate his players to achieve their best.

One quote sums up Dalglish perfectly. "He was just a comfort to talk to because there were no airs and graces about him, nothing like that. What you see is what you get and he's always said, to this present day, 'If there is anything at all that you need that you think I can help with, I will do it.'"

A family man, married to his wife Marina since 1974 and father of four children, he keeps his personal life private. Dalglish has faced his share of personal challenges. His wife was diagnosed with breast cancer but fortunately recovered and he continues to inspire others through his dedication and charity work, as for

example, his work not only for the cancer charity founded by his wife, but for children's causes around the world.

In 1985, Dalglish was awarded an OBE for his services to football, and in 2018, he became a Knight Bachelor for his services to football and to charity. The following are some of Dalglish's other awards:

Personal Awards:
▶ Football Writers' Association Footballer of the Year: 1985-86 (as manager);
▶ Premier League Manager of the Month, January 1994, November 1994

Club Awards:
▶ English League Cup: 1983-84.
▶ English First Division: 1985-86, 1987-88, 1989-90 (as manager);
▶ FA Cup: 1985-86, 1988-89 (as manager);
▶ FA Charity Shield: 1986, 1988, 1989, 1990 (as manager);
▶ Football League Super Cup: 1985-86 (as manager);
▶ European Super Cup: 1985-86 (as manager)

JÜRGEN KLOPP

CHARACTERISED BY HIS HIGH-ENERGY, PRESSING GAME

Jürgen Klopp is a German football manager, widely recognised for his impressive work as the head coach of Liverpool FC. Klopp joined Liverpool in October 2015, following the departure of Brendan Rodgers, and has since transformed the club into one of the most dominant teams in European football.

During his time at Liverpool, Klopp has led the team to several impressive victories, and included in his best games are: the famous 4-0 victory over FC Barcelona in the second leg of the Champions League semi-finals in 2019. Liverpool had lost the first leg 3-0, but an incredible performance from the team saw them win 4-0 at Anfield, securing their place in the final. Another of Klopp's impressive team achievements was the 4-3 victory over Borussia Dortmund in the Europa League quarter-finals in 2016. Liverpool were 3-1 down with 25 minutes left to play, but a remarkable comeback saw them win the game in the dying seconds. Finally, the 2-0 victory over Tottenham Hotspur in the Champions League final in 2019 was also a significant achievement for Klopp and his team. Fans probably thank him, too, for the game against Manchester City in the 2017-18 Premier League season in which Liverpool ended City's unbeaten run and displayed a Liverpool team at the top of their game.

Klopp's managerial and coaching style is characterised by his high-energy, pressing game, and his excellent man-management skills. He has a reputation for creating a strong team spirit and fostering a sense of togetherness among his players. Klopp's strengths also include his tactical flexibility, his ability to motivate his team, and his willingness to take risks. His players have praised his positive attitude and his unwavering belief in their abilities.

However, Klopp's coaching style has also faced some criticism. One of his weaknesses is his tendency to rely heavily on his first-team players, often neglecting to give younger players a chance. His teams have also been criticised for being susceptible to defensive errors, particularly from set-pieces. As his high-pressure tactics can lead to fatigue amongst the players it can result in a high risk of injury. But his style of play has been successful in bringing out the best in his players, allowing them to showcase their talents and abilities on the field. His tactical acumen has helped Liverpool overcome some of the toughest opponents in the world of football. Klopp has a unique ability to connect with his players on a personal level and create a sense of togetherness and camaraderie within the squad.

Klopp's success at Liverpool has also been due to his tactical flexibility and willingness to adapt his style of play to suit the strengths and weaknesses of his opponents.

But Klopp's achievements at Liverpool speak for themselves. He has won several major trophies, including the Champions League, the Premier League and the FIFA Club World Cup. Klopp has succeeded in building a team that has become known for their attacking flair, their high-energy style of play and their ability to win games under pressure.

The manager has built his reputation not just on his impressive coaching and managerial skills but also on his personal character. Described as passionate, charismatic and a great motivator, Klopp's personal qualities have helped him form a strong bond with his players and fans.

Despite criticism, his skill in identifying and developing young talent has been credited with giving opportunities to young players at Liverpool, such as Trent Alexander-Arnold, and players of the calibre of Sadio Mané, Virgil van Djik and Roberto Firmino are unsparing in their praise for his help. Klopp's willingness to trust and encourage young players has helped build a strong sense of unity and togetherness within the squad.

Klopp is also known for his philanthropic activities outside of football. He has supported a number of charitable causes and foundations, including the Liverpool-based food bank, Fans Supporting Foodbanks. Klopp's commitment to social causes and his willingness to use his platform to raise awareness and support for those in need have endeared him to fans and admirers around the world.

Away from football, Klopp had been married twice, and he and his wife Ulla have one son each from their previous marriages. Klopp has spoken publicly about the importance of his family and how they have helped him maintain a balanced perspective on life and thus made him greatly respected off the pitch

This means that Jürgen Klopp is not just a great football manager. His passion for the game, his commitment to social causes and his ability to inspire and motivate have made him a beloved figure in the world of football.

The following are some of Klopp's awards as Liverpool manager:

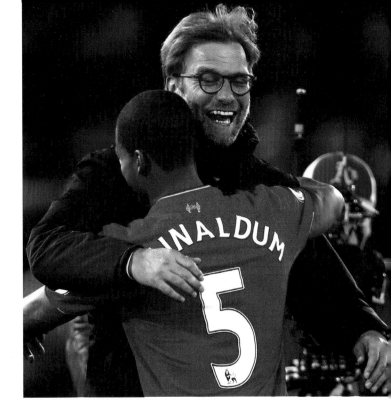

▲ Georginio Wijnaldum and Jürgen Klopp, celebrate victory during the Premier League match between Liverpool and Manchester City at Anfield on 31 December 2016

Personal Awards:
▶ The Best FIFA Men's Coach: 2019;
▶ LMA Hall of Fame: 2019;
▶ LMA Manager of the Year: 2019-20, 2021-22
▶ Premier League Manager of the Season: 2019-20, 2021-22;
▶ Premier League Manager of the Month: September 2016, December 2018, March 2019, August 2019, September 2019, November 2019, December 2019, January 2020, May 2021;
▶ BBC Sports Personality of the Year (Coach) 2020;
▶ Freedom of the City of Liverpool: 2022

Club Awards:
▶ Premier League: 2019-20;
▶ FA Cup: 2021-22;
▶ Football League Cup/EFL Cup: 2021-22;
▶ FA Community Shield: 2022;
▶ UEFA Champions League: 2018-19;
▶ UEFA Super Cup: 2019;
▶ FIFA Club World Cup: 2019

THE 10 GREATEST LFC TEAMS OF ALL TIME

I n Liverpool Football Club's long and illustrious history, many great teams have graced Anfield, captivating fans around the world with their skill, passion and determination and will never be forgotten. From the trailblazing sides of the 1970s to the iconic achievements of the 1980s and the modern-day successes under Jürgen Klopp, Liverpool has carved out a place in footballing history that is unparalleled. It is an impossible task to pick the best of the best, but these 10 provided drama, glamour and glory in equal measure.

▶ Teams from 1963-64 and 1983-84

▲ Liverpool celebrate with the European Cup, 30 June 1984

The squad of the 1983-84 season was definitely one of the greatest teams in the history of English football. Managed by Joe Fagan, the team won a historic treble, consisting of the then English First Division, the League Cup and the European Cup.

The team's tactical strength was their ability to play a high-pressing game, with a focus on quick, incisive passing and movement off the ball. The team's back line was a perfect blend of smooth play and steely defence led by the fortification of centre-back pairing of the elegant Alan Hansen building attacks from the back and fierce central defender Mark Lawrenson.

Liverpool's midfield during the 1983-84 season was a key part of the club's success. The midfield was typically made up of four players, with Graeme Souness playing in the centre of the field alongside Sammy Lee or Ronnie Whelan. Souness was the standout performer, with his tough tackling, vision and ability to control the game in midfield. This was also his last season for the club. He presented a major goal threat, scoring a total of 12 goals in all competitions during the season.

Liverpool's talented forwards were Ian Rush and Kenny Dalglish. Rush was outstanding, netting a total of 47 goals in all competitions during the season. Dalglish was a key figure both on and off the field, providing leadership and inspiration to the team.

But it was Ian Rush who took the honours as the player to see that season. The Welsh forward was in the form of his life during the 1983-84 season. Rush's ability to score goals from a variety of positions and in a variety of ways was a key reason for Liverpool's success during this period.

Liverpool's best games during the 1983-84 season came in the latter stages of the European Cup. Liverpool faced a tough test against Portuguese side Benfica but dominated the second leg with Rush, Craig Johnston and Ronnie Whelan scoring in a 4-1 victory.

Then, in the final against Roma, the match went to penalties, with Liverpool eventually winning 4-2 in the shoot-out to secure their fourth European Cup trophy.

They added that cup to the League Cup and a 1-0 victory over Everton, to end a magnificent season, which had also given them the league title.

LIVERPOOL ASCENDANT (2000-01)

The Liverpool team for the 2000-01 season was one of the most successful in the club's history, winning three major trophies and cementing their reputation as one of the best teams in Europe. Managed by Gérard Houllier, the team was built on a solid defensive foundation, with Sami Hyypiä and Stéphane Henchoz forming a formidable centre-back partnership. Behind them, the experienced Sander Westerveld provided a reliable presence in goal.

In midfield, usually made up of a combination of three or four players, was the combative Dietmar Hamann, a tough-tackling midfielder who provided a solid defensive shield in front of the back four in partnership with the inimitable Steven Gerrard.

Another of the key players in Liverpool's midfield that season was Scot Gary McAllister. McAllister was an experienced midfielder, who provided a calm presence and leadership in midfield with excellent understanding of the game and passing ability. He was also a set-piece specialist and scored several important goals throughout the season, including the first goal in the League Cup final penalty shoot-out. He was named Premier League Player of the Month for April 2001.

He and Hamann controlled the tempo of games and provided a platform for the attacking players.

The standout player for Liverpool that season was Michael Owen, who was just 21 years old at the time. Owen scored 24 goals in all competitions, including both goals in the FA Cup final against Arsenal, the second was a stunning solo effort that showcased his pace and skill, and Owen was named the World Soccer Player of the Year. His pace, skill and blistering finishing made him a constant threat to opposing defences and he played a pivotal role in the team's success, scoring crucial goals throughout the season.

One of the key strengths of the Liverpool team that season was their ability to win games by narrow margins. They were adept at grinding out results, with a solid defence and a scything attack. This was evident in their best games of the season, the first of which was the UEFA Cup final against Alaves: Liverpool won an incredible game 5-4 after extra time, with help from a golden goal from Delfí Geli scored in his own net. The FA Cup final against Arsenal was another classic match. Liverpool won 2-1.

▲ Michael Owen scores the first goal during the AXA sponsored 2001 FA Cup Final against Arsenal, 12 May 2001

◄ Liverpool celebrate winning the 2001 FA Cup

The Liverpool team of the 1985-86 season is regarded as one of the greatest football teams of all time. Led by player-manager Kenny Dalglish, Liverpool had a squad full of talented players who played with great tactical awareness and skill, winning a league and cup double that season. The team was, said Dalglish: "The best Liverpool side I've played in."

The tactical strength of the team was its ability to play with both flair and efficiency. This was a team that could dominate possession and create scoring opportunities through their quick and precise passing game. They also had a solid defence, which was able to withstand the pressure of opposing teams and keep clean sheets.

One of the best games of the season was undoubtedly the FA Cup final in May 1986 when Liverpool finished winners against Everton 3-1. It was a day to see Ian Rush at his scintillating best after a shock first goal by Gary Lineker for Everton and a lacklustre first 45 minutes by Liverpool.

But Rush was on hand to strike the first and third goals, speeding in to leave the keeper flailing for his first, speeding in again to hammer in the third, and Johnston was there, sloppily unmarked, to put away the second. With Bruce Grobbelaar magnificent in goal this was another wonderful Liverpool fightback.

In the domestic league, Liverpool won the title with a two-point lead over their nearest rivals, Everton again. One of their most spectacular games came in a 6-0 thrashing of Oxford United, and then walloping Coventry City 5-0 with Ronnie Whelan getting a hat-trick. The outstanding striker for Liverpool in the 1985-86 season was Ian Rush whose strengths and skills that made him one of the most dangerous strikers in the game at the time.

The strengths of the Liverpool team were evident throughout. The defence was anchored by Grobbelaar in goal with Alan Hansen and Mark Lawrenson indomitable at the back. Liverpool's midfield during produced well-balanced football and they possessed a range of skills and abilities, their collective efforts were crucial in the club's success that season. Ronnie Whelan's contributions in midfield were particularly notable, and Jan Mølby was a welcome new sensation in that area of the field.

▼ FA Cup Final, Alan Hansen and teammates celebrating with the trophy, 10 May 1986

Under the guidance of their manager, Bill Shankly, Liverpool went from an ageing, second-rate team to rising to claim the league championship.

One of the defining characteristics of this team was their tactical discipline and teamwork. Shankly had instilled a strong work ethic in his players, and they were feared for their pressing and hard-tackling style of play. This was backed up by a solid defensive unit that was anchored by the likes of Ron Yeats and Gerry Byrne.

The outstanding player of the season was undoubtedly striker Roger Hunt, who scored 31 goals in all competitions. Hunt's movement and finishing ability made him a constant threat to opposition defences, and he formed a lethal partnership with Ian St John, who scored 21, with forward Alf Arrowsmith also firing on all cylinders.

Liverpool's defensive record was also impressive with only 45 goals conceded in 42 league games. The defence for the 1963-64 season became almost impenetrable and provided the foundation for the team's success that year. Tommy Lawrence was the undisputed linchpin of the rearguard actors, using his physicality and aerial ability to dominate opposing forwards, pulling off crucial saves. Lawrence kept 133 clean sheets throughout his career.

In front of him, Byrne and Ronnie Moran, rarely beaten by a winger for pace and also a penalty expert, and Chris Lawler, a 41-goal right-back, were disciplined and organised.

The Liverpool midfield of the 1963-64 season was a formidable force led by the feisty centre-half Ron Yeats, the midfield providing a solid defensive platform from which the team could launch their attacks. Yeats was a commanding presence in the centre of the pitch, 6'

▲ Liverpool players celebrate in their dressing room at Anfield after clinching the League championship, 18 April 1964

2" tall, using his strength and aerial ability to break up opposition attacks and win possession. Gordon Milne was also pulling the strings in Liverpool's attacking play. Meanwhile, players such as Ian Callaghan and Peter Thompson provided pace and energy down the flanks.

Liverpool had started the season badly but when Ian Callaghan scored both goals in a 2-1 victory against Everton the tide turned and led to a run of five consecutive victories. With another four back-to-back wins the team reached the top spot. The league was won in a 5-0 romp against Arsenal, even though the final three games were best forgotten about.

LIVERPOOL REIGN SUPREME (1972-73)

iverpool FC's 1972-73 season was one of the most dominant campaigns in the club's richly layered history. Led by manager Bill Shankly, the reshaped Reds captured their eighth First Division title in style, finishing six points clear of rivals Arsenal after a season that included a record, 21 consecutive home wins in the league and the UEFA Cup.

The team's tactical strengths were built on a solid foundation of disciplined defending and dynamic attacking play. The defence, anchored by England international Ray Clemence in goal and with the skills of Larry Lloyd, Tommy Smith and Chris Lawler, was incredibly tough to break down, conceding just 42 goals in 42 league matches. Meanwhile, the midfield was marshalled by the influential captain and legendary midfielder, Ian Callaghan. Callaghan's ability to control the tempo of games and dictate the play was crucial to the team's success. Finally, the attack was spearheaded by the mercurial forward Kevin Keegan, who scored an impressive 22 league goals in the campaign, aided and abetted by the superb winger Steve Heighway. The team was renowned for its attacking spirit, and they scored an impressive 72 goals in 42 league matches, with their quick, dynamic attacking play causing problems for even the most resolute defences.

One of the most nail-biting games was the 3-2 win against Newcastle United, and the toughest the 2-0 win

▲ UEFA Cup Final second leg match in Munich. Borussia Mönchengladbach 2 v Liverpool 0. Celebrations for Liverpool as they win their first European trophy with Kevin Keegan carried on fans shoulders after they invaded the pitch, 23 May 1973

against Leeds United away from home. But vying for the most entertaining game was arguably Liverpool's 5-0 victory over Sheffield United. The Reds put on a scintillating display, with goals from Phil Boersma, Alec Lindsay, Heighway, Peter Cormack and Keegan. Who produced the best goal of the season — Emlyn Hughes against Wolves with a superb drive? Keegan's zipping header in the same match? Callaghan's ripper against Stoke City?

"Irrepressible" Kevin Keegan was without doubt the outstanding player of the season. The young forward was in sensational form, scoring 28 goals in all competitions and establishing himself as one of the most exciting players in English football.

The Liverpool team of 1972-73 will always be remembered for their dominant and stylish performances, but it was their togetherness and unity that really set them apart. As Shankly himself said: "The greatest thing about Liverpool is the team spirit. It's something you can't buy. You can't put your finger on it, but it's there."

L iverpool FC's 1976-77 season was one of the most successful in the club's history. Under the guidance of manager Bob Paisley, the Reds captured their first European Cup, as well as their 10th league title. Paisley's tactics relied on a compact defence, pressing midfielders and quick, incisive attacks to overwhelm opponents. The team's tactical discipline and versatility made them a formidable force both domestically and in Europe.

The unshakeable defence boasting Ray Clemence, widely regarded as one of the best goalkeepers of his generation, bolstered the team's tactical strengths and enabled the forwards to become a potent attacking force. This defence, led by the imposing centre-back duo of Emlyn Hughes and six-footer Phil Thompson, conceded just 33 goals in 42 league matches. Meanwhile, the midfield was controlled by the irreplaceable Ray Kennedy, Shankly's "great new player", tenacious Jimmy Case, the versatile and fierce Peter Cormack and the inimitable Ian Callaghan. Finally, forward Kevin Keegan, hard to pin down as ever, led the attack alongside ace striker John Toshack, the duo forming a lethal partnership upfront.

The best game of the season came with the European Cup final against Borussia Mönchengladbach. Played at the Stadio Olimpico in Rome, Liverpool produced a dominant performance, with goals from Terry McDermott, Tommy Smith and Phil Neal securing a memorable 3-1 victory.

Keegan was once again in a league of his own that season. The dynamic forward was in sensational form, scoring 20 league goals and providing numerous assists. His performances earned him the FWA Footballer of the Year award.

Yet it was Steve Heighway who pulled off the

▲ European lap of honour after beating Borussia Mönchengladbach, 1977

best league goal of the season once more with a strike against Tottenham Hotspur at Anfield. After a neat interchange of passes with Keegan, Heighway unleashed a thunderous left-footed shot from outside the box that fired into the net.

The Liverpool team of 1976-77 will always be remembered for their success both domestically and in Europe. As Bob Paisley himself said: "We didn't have to dominate the ball all the time, but when we had it, we made sure we used it well." The team's combination of a solid defence, a hardworking midfield and a lethal attack often made them unbeatable, and they will always be remembered as one of the greatest Liverpool sides of all time.

The Liverpool 1984-85 season was a rollercoaster ride for a team that deserves mention and respect for trying so hard in a year of tragedy and mental stress (when 39 Juventus fans died in Belgium), coming so close to trophies so often, nonetheless, but not quite managing the final inches; second in the league, runners-up in the European Cup, the European Super Cup and the Intercontinental Cup. Lady Luck was not with a team that had several outstanding players such as Ian Rush, Kenny Dalglish and Alan Hansen. The team travelled through a bad patch with seven games back-to-back without a win in the league and not one win against any of the title contenders.

Yet the team's attacking, thrilling football with flair, domination in midfield and defensive solidity was on display in one of the best games of the season; an exhilarating 4-3 win over Chelsea in the league, with Steve Nicol scoring two, Rush and Ronnie Whelan one apiece, Whelan's coming after just four minutes.

Manager Joe Fagan's tactics were based on a fast and fluid attacking style in games played with high tempo, and pressurising opponents relentlessly so that they would find it difficult to build attacks. One particular tactic was that the backs were allowed to overlap in

▲ December 1984. Liverpool training session in Tokyo

support of forward movement thus opening up space for Liverpool's midfielders and forwards to explore with more freedom.

The team put in a mesmerising display in a 5-0 thrashing of West Bromwich Albion, their intelligent, skilful and adventurous football showing the superb quality that made the team one of the best in the world. Dalglish was absolutely scintillating pushing through accurate and expert passes, his performance culminating in a 20-yard dynamite goal scored with his left foot. Bruce Grobbelaar, too, was in fine form to prevent the opposition from spoiling his clean sheet while John Wark did damage with a hat-trick at the other end. Nicol had started the rout after just six minutes.

It was undoubtedly painful going down to Juventus in the European Cup final, losing to a single penalty having already ceded the European Super Cup to Juventus by two goals in January 1985. A reflective Joe Fagan said: "We may not have come away with any trophies, but we still played some fantastic football and showed great spirit and determination throughout the season."

The season was a remarkable one for Liverpool FC, as they lifted the Champions League trophy in one of the greatest comebacks in the history of the competition. Under the guidance of manager Rafael Benítez, the team showed incredible tactical strength, resilience and fighting spirit throughout the campaign.

The team's best performance arrived, fortunately, with the Champions League final against AC Milan in Istanbul. Liverpool found themselves 3-0 down at half-time, but a stunning second-half comeback saw them level the scores at 3-3, with goals from Steven Gerrard, Vladimír Šmicer and Xabi Alonso. The match went to penalties, where Liverpool goalkeeper Jerzy Dudek made two crucial saves to secure a 3-2 victory. Dudek had already proved his agility with an incredible double save against Milan's Andriy Shevchenko, denying him twice in quick succession.

Liverpool's tactical strengths relied on a solid defence, hard-working midfield and attacking flair. The backline, led by centre-backs Jamie Carragher and Sami Hyypiä, was strong and disciplined. In midfield, the likes of Gerrard, Xabi Alonso and Dietmar Hamann provided the work rate and creativity needed to control games and launch attacks. Up at the front, the attacking trio of Milan Baroš, Luis García and Harry Kewell combined pace, skill and the goalscoring threat.

One man was outstanding in the 2004-05 season; Steven Gerrard. The Liverpool captain was a driving force for the team, scoring crucial goals in the league and Champions League, including the first goal in the final against AC Milan. His leadership, skill and determination were key factors in the team's success that season and his stunning long-range strike against Olympiacos in the Champions League group stage, one of his best, secured Liverpool's place in the knockout rounds.

Manager Rafael Benítez's tactical acumen and motivational skills were evident throughout the campaign and key to Liverpool's success in that season of 2004-05. These skills were never more evident than when he masterminded the stunning comeback in the Champions League final.

"It was just a remarkable achievement from the Liverpool team that year," said former Liverpool striker Michael Owen. "They showed incredible heart, belief and determination to come back from three goals down in the final, and it will go down as one of the greatest moments in the history of the club." the greatest Liverpool sides of all time.

▲ Steven Gerrard proudly lifts the Champions League trophy in 2005

◀ The Fab Three — Mohamed Salah, Roberto Firmino and Sadio Mané

Europe second to none.

Behind them, Alex Oxlade-Chamberlain and captain Jordan Henderson dominated midfield, and Trent Alexander-Arnold's creativity and distribution in defence complemented Virgil van Dijk's physical prowess and vision in anticipating the game flow. The contributions of these four were essential to Liverpool's success throughout their 2021-22 campaign resulting in just 26 goals scored against them as their forwards tucked away 94.

In a season where Manchester United were humiliated twice 5-0 and 4-0, Leeds United downed 6-0 and Arsenal 4-0 and 2-0, it's hard to choose the best of many impressive games. As former England striker Alan Shearer said: "Liverpool are a team that can beat anyone on their day. They have a strong defence, a potent attack and a midfield that works tirelessly for the team."

But let's go for Liverpool's 5-0 home win against Watford in October to focus on the sheer chutzpah of the Liverpool forwards. The front three of Salah, Mané and Firmino combined for all five goals, with Mané opening the scoring on the eighth minute, Firmino bagging a hat-trick, and Salah providing absolutely stunning passing and netting an even more stunning solo effort that saw him dribble and confuse several defenders before slotting the ball into the back of the net.

Both those skills were to the fore against Manchester United in April 2022 as well, with Mané and Salah combining to show how they destroy defences with Salah's daring, speed and a delicate chip gaining him another goal.

Liverpool's 2021-22 season was a challenging (as the club navigated through a number of injuries) but hugely successful one, and the team was just pipped at the post by one point in the Premier League coming closer to a quadruple than any other team in English league history. But for the ninth time in their illustrious journey, Liverpool won the League Cup, a tournament record, and the FA Cup, the eighth time they had raised that silverware.

Jürgen Klopp employed his relentless *Gegenpressing* philosophy, which was heavily dependent on the work rate and fitness of the entire team — so that each player was ready to spring into action on or off the ball — paired with a killer instinct to make the most of the mistakes by the unsettled opposition. With Mohamed Salah, Roberto Firmino and Sadio Mané, Klopp could boast an attacking line-up in

A BREATH-TAKING DISPLAY (1987-88)

After finishing second in the league to their arch-rivals Everton the previous year, the team was determined to bounce back and reclaim their title. Guided by manager Kenny Dalglish's tactical intelligence, Liverpool put in a stellar performance that saw them win the league nine points clear of Manchester United. As former Liverpool midfielder Ray Houghton said of Dalglish's leadership: "He was a great motivator and got the best out of everybody... He knew how to get the team going and how to win." Ian Rush's departure had brought in £3.2m in transfer fees and Dalglish's eye for talent proved to be unparalleled in what came to be known as Liverpool's "Samba season".

The thrills abounded in one of the best matches of the season. What had been a forgone conclusion with the Reds 3-1 up against Manchester United turned into a nail-biting encounter, thanks to bad luck, that ended 3-3. Nonetheless, the first half of the match showcased Liverpool's tactical strengths, as they adapted their style of play to break down United and force their defence onto the back foot.

Liverpool's strength lay in their balanced squad, with world-class players in every area of the pitch. The pivots of the defence were Alan Hansen and Steve

Nicol (Nicol scored six goals in his first six league games) while the midfield boasted the inventive skills of Steve McMahon and John Barnes. John Aldridge and Peter Beardsley formed a deadly partnership on the attack that terrorised opposition defences.

John Barnes was on searing form this season. The winger with wings was voted PFA Players' Player of the Year and FWA Footballer of the Year and was tireless in helping Liverpool achieve success, scoring crucial goals and providing countless assists. However, the outstanding player of the season was undoubtedly John Aldridge, who finished as the team's top scorer with 29 goals in all competitions. Aldridge's goalscoring instincts and unerring finishing were key to Liverpool's success, as he consistently found the back of the net with memorable goals throughout the season displaying moments of individual brilliance that epitomised his importance to the team. Never more so than in the 5-0 walloping of Nottingham Forest, when Aldridge put away two goals and Liverpool were at their unstoppable best.

THE 10 GREATEST LFC TEAMS OF ALL TIME

GAMES

THE 10 GREATEST LFC GAMES OF ALL TIME

Who dares to select the greatest games of all time and especially only 10 of them? Impossible, of course. But as Liverpool teams know, he who dares wins, so here we go with a very subjective 10 greatest, evidence of what Liverpool FC are capable of. Superlatives abound as some of the greatest names in Liverpool history take to the field to produce the most extraordinary, momentous and thrilling games in the club's rich history.

▶ The games Liverpool FC turned the footballing world red!

Competition: European Cup
Teams: Liverpool vs Club Brugge
Final score: Liverpool 1-0 Club Brugge
Date: 10 May 1978
Venue: Wembley Stadium, London
Goalscorer: Dalglish (64')
Liverpool Man of the Match: Graeme Souness

▲ Alan Hansen, Kenny Dalglish and Graeme Souness celebrate with the cup

iverpool claimed their second European Cup the first British club to do so. It was a historic moment for Liverpool, who had become a dominant force in English football under the management of Bob Paisley.

Club Brugge were a formidable opponent and a tough team to beat. They were a disciplined and well-organised team, and they were able to keep possession for long periods of time without losing their shape and employed offside tactics to keep Liverpool at bay. This made it difficult for Liverpool to create chances besides putting pressure on their defence.

Liverpool's own tough defence kept the Belgians out and thus enabled the victory. Liverpool came close on numerous occasions with superb flowing moves but Brugge keeper Birger Jensen was on sparkling form to deny the Reds every time. Brugge attempted to stifle the Liverpool attack using man-to-man marking and honed their offside tactics as the match progressed. But Graeme Souness soon had the measure of that and floated beautiful passes to the front that the attackers

could latch on to helped by Terry McDermott, whose sense of position and awareness on the ball was crucial to Liverpool's offensive game.

Kenny Dalglish played a central role in Liverpool's attacking efforts, with his runs and passes creating several chances for his teammates. Nevertheless, by half time the Reds had still been unable to make their intelligent football pay dividends, and the attempts and near-misses piled up. It was exciting football, though; Ray Kennedy volleyed it, Jimmy Case pounded it, David Fairclough dribbled it and Alan Hansen headed it; all to no avail.

In the second half, Steve Heighway was brought on and the Liverpool game opened out with more width.

It was Souness, however, who was the linchpin in the successful move. By holding on to the ball just long enough when he spotted that his teammates might be offside, he paved the way for Dalglish to get into position and then made the pass through the defence. Dalglish tore away and onto it and with a cool-headed and cheeky chip across the face of the goal he scored the winner.

Phil Thompson saved Liverpool's blushes with a save off the line as the game drew to a close. But Liverpool's victory was founded on a solid defensive display and efficient use of possession with Bob Paisley's tactics crucial, as Liverpool nullified the Club Brugge attack and played with discipline and commitment throughout.

GERRARD INSPIRES FIGHTBACK

Competition: UEFA Champions League

Teams: Liverpool vs Olympiacos

Date: 8 December 2004

Venue: Anfield Stadium, Liverpool

Final score: Liverpool 3-1 Olympiacos

Goalscorers:

Liverpool: Sinama-Pongoll (47'); Neil Mellor (81')

Gerrard (86')

Olympiacos: Rivaldo (27')

Liverpool Man of the Match: Steven Gerrard

▲ Steven Gerard celebrates scoring to make it 3-1

Liverpool needed to win by two goals or by a score of 1-0 to progress to the knockout stages of the competition.

The match started with an attacking display from Liverpool, but they were unable to find the back of the net. It was Olympiacos who took the lead through an excellent Rivaldo free-kick in the 27th minute. That left Liverpool needing three goals to secure their place in the next round. Liverpool's tactics were weighted towards an attacking game with the team pushing forward with intensity and looking to score from the beginning of the match. However, they were forced to adjust their tactics after conceding the first goal, shifting to a more aggressive attacking strategy to try and overcome the two-goal deficit. But by half time, the situation had not changed.

In the second half, Liverpool put on a spirited performance, pushing forward relentlessly. It was Florent Sinama-Pongolle who put Liverpool back into the game as he found space under pressure to bang in the cross. Liverpool went all out for the second goal keeping up the pressure and when the Greek team failed to clear a fabulous Pongolle cross from their box, substitute Neil Mellor was razor-sharp on the spot to take a rebound and thump the ball in for the Liverpool second.

Liverpool were relentless and when Mellor "nodded the ball softly to Steven Gerrard, the midfielder let loose a classic Gerrard shot from 20 yards out, absolutely blasting the ball with a steam-hammer drive past the keeper. Liverpool had completed a stunning comeback and despite suffering goals by Milan Baroš and Gerrard disallowed for prior fouls Liverpool put on a fighting display and it was Gerrard they had to thank from the outset as the "guarantor of accurate, high-tempo attacking".

Liverpool's performance was full of offensive intent, and they produced some beautiful football throughout the match. Despite going behind to a stunning goal, Liverpool never gave up and continued to push forward ruthlessly.

The key to Liverpool's success was their fighting spirit and never-say-die attitude, which led to their incredible comeback, particularly in the closing stages of the match and Liverpool's perseverance, spirit and attacking intent in the face of adversity marked a significant moment in the club's history. This match remains one of the most memorable occasions in modern Liverpool history.

THRILLING TORTURE

Competition: UEFA Cup, Final

Date: 16 May 2001

Teams: Liverpool vs Deportivo Alavés

Venue: Westfalenstadion, Dortmund, Germany

Final score: Liverpool 5-4 Deportivo Alavés (a.e.t.)

Goalscorers:

Liverpool: Babbel (4'), Gerrard (16'), McAllister (41', 116'), Fowler (73')

Deportivo Alavés: Alonso (26'), Moreno (47', 49'), Cruyff (88')

Liverpool Man of the Match: Gary McAllister

▲ Liverpool players celebrating with the UEFA Cup following their thrilling 5-4 victory over Alaves in 2001

Liverpool and underdogs Deportivo Alavés produced an exhilarating and unforgettable game, both teams displaying superb attacking creativity and defensive resilience. Alavés was particularly lethal on the counter-attack with the pace and skill of their forwards causing problems for Liverpool.

Gérard Houllier's tactics were based on Liverpool's attacking strength. Playing a 4-4-2 formation with an emphasis on getting the ball forward quickly and creating scoring opportunities, his tactics were successful but also left the defence exposed at times resulting in a high-scoring game that could have gone either way.

Liverpool were ahead just three minutes into the game when Markus Babbel, slipping the defenders, headed home a floating cross.

In the 16th minute, a young Steven Gerrard announced himself to the world with a terrific run and stunning goal from inside the box that helped set Liverpool on their way to victory.

Liverpool looked to be in control, but Alavés managed to pull a goal back through Iván Alonso in the 28th minute when Alonso got away from Babbel, rising up well at the far post to nod in Cosmin Contra's cross.

When Michael Owen was brought down by the keeper, the penalty added a third goal to Liverpool's tally.

The second half saw a flurry of goals though it was Alavés who started the half the better of the two sides. Contra crossed from the right side of the field into the penalty area, and Javi Moreno got to it first to beat Sander Westerveld and make the scoreline 3-2.

Alavés equalised in the 50th minutes as Moreno sent through a blistering shot.

Dietmar Hamann was the anchor of the Liverpool midfield, playing in a defensive midfield role while Gary McAllister was the creative force of the midfield providing incisive passes. Then, creating one of the game's momentous moments, Robbie Fowler darted across in front of the defenders to score an audacious goal giving Liverpool the lead again.

However, Alavés were not done yet. It was a team whose strength lay in their attack with Jordi Cruyff lethal on the counter-attack, particularly impressive and causing all manner of problems for the Liverpool defence, got his head to the ball to even the scores once more.

The additional 30 minutes were full of tense drama, but Liverpool eventually emerged on top — in a cruel manner thanks to a "golden goal", an own goal headed in from Alavés' midfielder Delfi Geli.

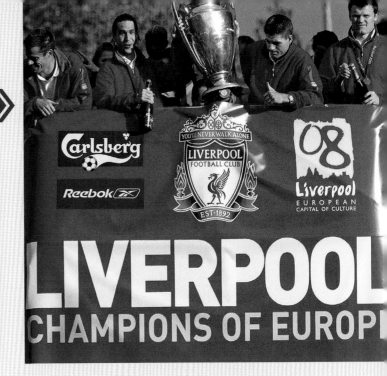

THE INCREDIBLE COMEBACK

Competition: UEFA Champions League, Final

Date: 25 May 2005

Venue: Atatürk Olympic Stadium, Istanbul, Turkey

Final score: Liverpool 3-3 AC Milan (Liverpool won 3-2 on penalties)

Goalscorers:

Liverpool: Gerrard (54'), Šmicer (56'), Alonso (60')

AC Milan: Maldini (1'), Crespo (39', 44')

Liverpool Man of the Match: Steven Gerrard

t was an unforgettable night in Istanbul in what transpired to be one of the greatest comebacks in football history as Liverpool overturned a 3-0 half-time deficit.

Manager Rafael Benítez made an unfortunate team selection by excluding Dietmar Hamann and Igor Biscan at the start, men who had been so successful in the campaign in Europe.

Liverpool started the match poorly and found themselves struggling to contain the AC Milan forwards. In contrast, Milan showcased their quality and strength as a team from the outset.

Milan benefitted from experienced players, tactical flexibility and the ability to switch between different formations and styles of play to start the game strongly, scoring the opening goal in just 51 seconds. The Italians then completely dominated the game.

At half-time, it seemed as though Milan were cruising to a comfortable victory having already scored three goals. However, Liverpool were not going down without a fight and the fightback began after half-time, with Steven Gerrard playing a pivotal role.

Gerrard scored Liverpool's first goal on 54 minutes, rising to the cross to thump in the ball with his head sparking a stunning comeback from Benítez's side. The momentum of the game had completely shifted

▲ Liverpool players hold up the Champions' League trophy to thousands of fans gathered to welcome them home, May 2005

in Liverpool's favour. Milan now struggled to contain Liverpool's attacking play, and also showed signs of tiredness and frustration as the game went on.

The Reds' second goal came just two minutes later with Vladimír Šmicer replacing Harry Kewell and scoring from a drive outside of the box after a clever pass from Gerrard. It was Šmicer's first goal for Liverpool, a long-range shot that rocketed beneath Dida to make it 3-2. The audacity and accuracy of the shot brought a goal that truly ignited Liverpool's comeback.

The equaliser came after Dida saved Xabi Alonso's spot-kick, but the Spanish midfield man followed up and fired the ball into the back of the net to level the scores with Milan's defenders looking on in stunned disbelief.

Despite this, Milan still had some chances to win the game in the second half and in extra time, especially through Andriy Shevchenko, who had several close-range efforts saved by Liverpool goalkeeper Jerzy Dudek. However, Dudek's saves and Liverpool's resilient defence meant that the game ultimately went to penalties.

DOMINANT REDS DISMANTLE UNITED

Competition: Premier League

Teams: Liverpool vs Manchester United

Date: 6 March 2011

Venue: Anfield Stadium, Liverpool

Final score: Liverpool 3-1 Manchester United

Goalscorers:

Liverpool: Kuyt (34', 39', 65')

Manchester United: Hernández (90')

Liverpool Man of the Match: Luis Suarez

Delivering a superb performance against their most bitter rivals Manchester United, the Reds' passionate and disciplined performance showcased their determination to dominate in all aspects of the game.

In March 2011, Manchester United were sitting at the top of the Premier League table.

Liverpool started the game with their usual 4-4-2 formation, with Dirk Kuyt up front alongside Luis Suárez. The Reds dominated right from the kick-off and took the lead after a superb Suárez went jigging brilliantly past three defenders for Kuyt to score. Buoyed by the early goal, Liverpool continued to control the game, with a strong midfield and impeccable defence. United struggled to respond, but their attacks were met with swift counter-attacks from Liverpool. And then Liverpool were two ahead from a header by Kuyt.

United's efforts in the second half were thwarted by an equally strong Liverpool defence and then it was Uruguayan Suárez who provided Kuyt with the chance to clock up a hat-trick. In the 65th minute when his free-kick was parried by the United keeper and Kuyt pounced to make it a hat-trick.

The performance of Liverpool's midfield trio of Steven Gerrard, Jay Spearing and Raul Meireles deserve mention for what was an exceptional

▲ Dirk Kuyt celebrates scoring his team's second goal

performance. They controlled the midfield, pressing high up the pitch to win possession and distributing the ball effectively to create chances for the front three.

Liverpool's defence, too, was solidly reliable throughout the game, with Jamie Carragher and Martin Škrtel making crucial interceptions and clearances to keep Liverpool ticking.

One of Kenny Dalglish's key tactical decisions was to give his team the freedom to attack their opponents from different angles. The front three players swapped positions frequently, making it difficult for United's defenders to mark them effectively. Additionally, when Liverpool lost possession, the players immediately pressed their opponents to win the ball back high up the pitch. The manager employed a diamond technique. In this formation, Liverpool played with two strikers up front and a midfield diamond with a holding midfielder and Steven Gerrard at the tip, and Jordan Henderson and Kuyt on the flanks. The team would often look to play a possession-based game with Gerrard providing creativity and drive from midfield and they dominated to such an extent that Andy Carroll could be sent on as a substitute without fearing that his thigh injury would be exacerbated by too much effort.

DYNAMIC LIVERPOOL DISSECT ARSENAL

Competition: **Premier League**

Teams: **Liverpool vs Arsenal**

Date: **29 December 2018**

Venue: **Anfield Stadium, Liverpool**

Final score: **Liverpool 5-1 Arsenal**

Goalscorers:

Liverpool: **Firmino (14', 16'), Mané (32', 45+2'), Salah (45')**

Arsenal: **Maitland-Niles (11')**

Liverpool Man of the Match: **Roberto Firmino**

▲ Roberto Firmino scores his side's second goal

Liverpool produced a true display of attacking prowess and impenetrable defence with gameplay both fluid and dynamic, with their front trio of Roberto Firmino, Sadio Mané and Mohamed Salah causing trouble for Arsenal's defence throughout the game. Liverpool conceded an early goal by Ainsley Maitland-Niles after a well-placed cross from Alex Iwobi, but responded swiftly with back-to-back strikes from Firmino within 90 seconds as he headed towards his hat-trick. His first was down to Lady luck when Arsenal attempted a clearance in their own box and the ball rebounded favourably for Firmino, who popped his certain strike, a no-look goal, into an empty net.

Firmino then created one of the game's highlight moments to put away an incredible second goal his first-class technique ending a move that saw him thrillingly jiggle past two tackles before unleashing a thumping shot into the bottom corner.

Liverpool continued to dominate the game, swarming forward in the style that had become their trademark and producing sizzling moments and some great moves, including a stunning back-heel from Firmino to set up Salah's goal. They also had some clever passes and combinations that kept Arsenal's defence guessing.

Mané added a third goal for the home side in the 32nd minute when Arsenal cleared a corner to Andy Robertson on halfway and his long ball forward was passed across the box by Salah for Mané to control the bouncing ball with a gentle tap and put the Reds further ahead.

Salah made it 4-1 in first-half injury-time when he was brought down, clumsily fouled by Sokratis, and then rifled a penalty past Bernd Leno.

The icing on the cake came when Salah was brought down again, and Firmino made no mistake with the second spot-kick either for number five.

Jürgen Klopp had reason to be pleased, his tactics were perfectly executed on the day. Liverpool dominated possession in midfield and pressurised Arsenal's defence, creating numerous opportunities to score. Liverpool's defenders and midfielders quickly closed down space and prevented the opposition from creating any significant chances.

"We were really good and did exactly what we wanted to do. We wanted to press them and cut off their build-up. They pressed us as well so it was wild. But then when you get the ball you need to calm down," said Klopp.

LIVERPOOL STUN BARCELONA

Competition: Champions League

Teams: Liverpool vs FC Barcelona

Date: 7 May 2019

Venue: Anfield Stadium, Liverpool

Final score: Liverpool 4-0 FC Barcelona

Goalscorers: Origi (7', 79'), Wijnaldum (54', 56')

Liverpool Man of the Match: Georginio Wijnaldum

Liverpool produced a performance that was nothing short of extraordinary. After losing the first leg 3-0, Liverpool needed a miracle to progress to the final, and their performance was one of the greatest in the history of the Champions League.

Liverpool got off to a cracking start in the seventh minute, when Divock Origi quickly followed up a great save by the keeper from Jordan Henderson to convert the rebound and start Liverpool's fightback.

FC Barcelona seemed to be caught off guard by Liverpool's physical intensity, pressing and quick passing game, and they couldn't react fast enough to keep Liverpool at bay.

Barcelona's strength, though, was their attacking prowess, and they boasted one of the best players in the world, Lionel Messi, who almost scored several times.

Then the nail biting began as Liverpool continued to push forward and were dominant throughout the first half, creating numerous chances to score but failing to do so. At half-time the score was still 1-0.

In the second half, Liverpool came out even stronger and Georginio Wijnaldum was the hero of the night, scoring two goals in just two minutes to level the tie. His first goal came as he raced into the box to take a long pass, thundering the ball into the net, goalkeeper Marc-André ter Stegen left floundering.

▲ Georginio Wijnaldum of Liverpool celebrates after scoring his team's third goal during the UEFA Champions League semi-final second leg match at Anfield on 7 May 2019

Two minutes later, the Liverpool man was at it again sailing up above two defenders to take the lofted cross and head the ball powerfully and beautifully to leave the goalkeeper flailing again for the third goal.

Meanwhile, Alisson was magnificent in the Liverpool goal, pulling of some spectacular quick-reaction saves including a Messi drive to keep the Spaniards out.

Then came the low corner that rocked Barcelona. It was perfectly placed by Trent Alexander-Arnold, who saw the chance, dropping the ball just outside the penalty area to where Origi had found a place clear of defenders to smack the ball in between the goalie and defender.

Jürgen Klopp's tactics had been spot-on for the game, as his players restricted Barcelona's ever-dangerous Lionel Messi from having any significant influence on the game. Liverpool's midfield three of James Milner, Henderson and Wijnaldum controlled the midfield battle, and Alexander-Arnold and Andy Robertson, Liverpool's full-backs, were a constant threat down the flanks.

REAL MADRID OUTCLASSED

Competition: **Champions League**
Date: **10 March 2009**
Venue: **Anfield Stadium, Liverpool**
Final score: **Liverpool 4-0 Real Madrid**
Goalscorers: **Torres (16'), Gerrard (28', 47'), Dossena (88')**
Liverpool Man of the Match: **Fernando Torres**

The Liverpool team played with great determination and skill to convincingly beat Real Madrid, with many claiming this was one of the team's finest performances in recent history. Rafael Benítez's team dominated in an inspired and stunning start from Liverpool forcing Madrid keeper Casillas into making two world-class saves in the opening minutes. Fernando Torres, who was playing against his former club, was the star of the first-half show, eventually scoring in the 16th minute to put Liverpool in control, latching onto a superb pass from Xabi Alonso and coolly slotting past the Madrid goalkeeper Iker Casillas. The best goal of the match.

A Liverpool penalty in the 28th minute slammed home by Steven Gerrard, more misery for Madrid's lackluster performers.

In the second half, Real Madrid brought on Marcelo after the interval to replace what was a very subdued Arjen Robben. But it was all made fairly irrelevant just two minutes later when Gerrard struck again. Gerrard darted forwards into space to track the ball as it fell towards him and tap the rebound from the ground high into the net with spot-on precision and high skill.

Madrid struggled to cope with Liverpool's fast-paced attacking style and were denied any opportunity to mould attacks or bring order to their play, Liverpool

▲ Steven Gerrard of Liverpool celebrates with teammate Fernando Torres after scoring during the UEFA Champions League Round of Sixteen, second leg match between Liverpool and Real Madrid at Anfield on 10 March 2009

underlining their vast superiority when they completed a surgical move for the fourth goal. Javier Mascherano saw the chance opening up as he sped forward to make a long and accurate cross-field pass, which a surging Andrea Dossena picked up to drive the ball into the net.

Real Madrid had claimed nine Champions League/European Cup titles before the 2009 match. Yet Real Madrid players were sloppy in possession, misplacing passes and failing to control the ball at important moments. The defenders looked disorganised and struggled to cope with Liverpool's pressing style and fast-paced attack.

Manager Benítez's tactics were well thought out and brilliantly carried through. He employed intense pressing actions to disrupt Real Madrid's possession and prevent them from settling into a rhythm. "I said to the players before the game that they could make history. They played with pride, passion and determination, and gave everything on the pitch. It was a great night for Liverpool football club."

LIVERPOOL'S EPIC RESURRECTION

Competition: FA Cup, Final

Date: 13 May 2006

Teams: Liverpool vs West Ham United

Venue: Millennium Stadium, Cardiff

Final score: Liverpool 3-3 West Ham United

(Liverpool won 3-1 on penalties)

Goalscorers:

Liverpool: Cissé (32'), Gerrard (54', 90+1')

West Ham United: Carragher (21', own goal),

Ashton (28'), Konchesky (64')

Liverpool Man of the Match: Steven Gerrard

▲ The teams line up for what will become an epic match

The 2006 FA Cup final was a rollercoaster of emotions for Liverpool and West Ham United fans. The game acquired the nickname, "the Gerrard Final".

Liverpool, who had already won the competition a record seven times, faced a West Ham side looking to win their first major trophy since the 1980s.

West Ham came out fighting and put Liverpool on the back foot with quick attacks and creativity in midfield. Then Jamie Carragher inadvertently put a cross into his own net giving West Ham the lead after just 21 minutes. West Ham often looked the better team and pressed on with the attacks, to be rewarded on the 28th minute when Pepe Reina couldn't hold a tame shot from Matthew Etherington, fumbled the ball at the feet of Dean Ashton, who pounced to prod in the ball.

Liverpool's recovery began in the 32nd minute when Gerrard saw the chance and floated the ball over the defence right to the feet of Djibril Cissé. The French striker met Gerrard's dropping ball on the volley to fire a hard shot past Shaka Hislop.

Now 2-1 down, Liverpool manager Rafa Benítez adjusted his tactics for the second half. He switched to a more aggressive 3-4-3 formation, which put West Ham's defence under more pressure and allowed Liverpool the chance to play more attacking football.

Steven Gerrard punished the West Ham defence when he was left in a huge space in front of goal. He unleashed a ferocious right-foot shot for a stunning long-range goal in the 54th minute, which brought Liverpool level.

But a long-range strike from Paul Konchesky gave West Ham the lead again. His rising ball caught Liverpool goalkeeper Pepe Reina off guard and sailed over his head and into the net.

As the 90-minute mark approached Gerrard was one-third of the way up the pitch when he received the ball as it bounced out of the West Ham defence. Unexpectedly, he took one look and let loose with a blistering shot from his right foot. The ball scythed through defenders and attackers alike and left the keeper prostrate on the ground to make it three all. An extraordinary shot.

Finally, Reina shone in the penalty shoot-out to deliver Liverpool the FA Cup.

The final was a testament to the Red's fighting spirit and resilience, able to draw level and then stay focused and win.

THE RED REVENGERS

Stan Collymore scores a dramatic last-minute winning goal during the FA Carling Premiership match between Liverpool and Newcastle United played at Anfield. Liverpool won the match 4-3, 3 April 1996

Competition: **Premier League**
Date: 3 April 1996
Teams: Liverpool vs Newcastle United
Venue: Anfield, Liverpool
Final score: Liverpool 4-3 Newcastle United
Goalscorers:
Liverpool: Fowler (2', 55'), Collymore (68', 90+2')
Newcastle United: Ferdinand (10'), Ginola (14'),
Asprilla (57')
Liverpool Man of the Match: Stan Collymore

The match had fans on the edge of their seats from start to finish. Both teams were in contention for the league title, and the high-stakes match did not disappoint.

Liverpool started the game on the front foot and took the lead in the second minute when Robbie Fowler latched onto a cross from Stan Collymore and headed the ball down and past Newcastle United goalkeeper Pavel Srníček. However, Newcastle quickly responded with an equaliser just eight minutes later. Les Ferdinand twisted around the Liverpool defenders to whack in a cross.

The game continued to ebb and flow, but Liverpool found themselves behind just four minutes later through David Ginola.

Two of the most lethal strikers in the league, Fowler and Collymore put their surgical finishing and ability to create chances out of nothing on full display for the Reds although Fowler waited until the 55th minute to finish a superb flowing move and thump the ball into the net.

Undeterred Newcastle fought back immediately and Faustino Asprilla put his team back in the lead two minutes later when he was left all alone to charge through and strike a beautiful volley into the net.

Liverpool manager, Roy Evans, employed an attacking and high-pressing style of play that put Newcastle under constant pressure, and sure enough after 10 minutes Collymore was on target when a terrific floating pass dropped right in front of the keeper for the Liverpool man to slot in.

"It was a fantastic game of football," said Evans, "and I think it showed what Liverpool is all about — attacking football, great spirit and a never-say-die attitude."

The game was tied at 3-3, but there was still more drama to come. In the 90th minute, Liverpool launched a counter-attack, and John Barnes cleverly launched the ball over to Collymore running in on the edge of the box. Collymore surged into the free space before firing in his magnificent second.

Dynamic and creative with the likes of Barnes, Jamie Redknapp and Steve McManaman instrumental in driving the team forward and creating chances for the forwards, Liverpool attacked with pace and skill, and the game was played at a frenetic pace. With several near misses and last-ditch tackles, the intensity never let up.